MUNI PHOTOGRAPHS

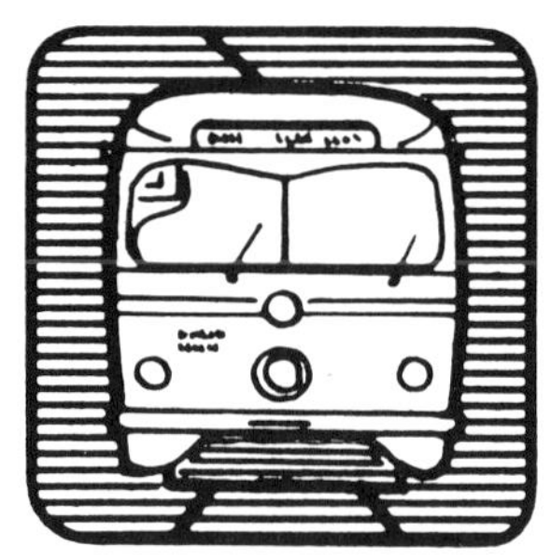

THE PHOTOGRAPHY OF
JEFFREY MOREAU

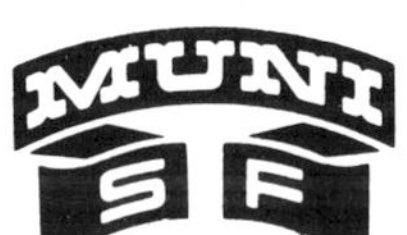

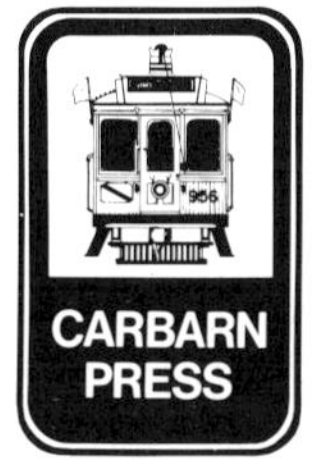

MUNI PHOTOGRAPHS

Library of Congress Catalog Card No. 91-72515

I.S.B.N. 0-934406-04-9

Printed in Hong Kong

First Printing: June 1991

●

COVER PHOTOGRAPHS

FRONT COVER

UPPER LEFT: L.R.V. No. 1213 is shown outbound on Market Street, between Kearny St. and Grant Ave., on July 10, 1983, during the first San Francisco Historic Trolley Festival. Light patronage of this modern car caused its early withdrawl from the lineup of electric railway vehicles operating as a part of the festival.

LOWER RIGHT: Vintage San Francisco Municipal Railway electric cars, No. 178 - on the left - and No. 1 - on the right - pose on March 13, 1982, at the old Geneva Carbarn on the occasion of an excursion trip aboard car No. 178 sponsored by the author.

REAR COVER

Historic trolley coach No. 776 poses westbound under line No. 24's twin wires on 30th Street, alongside L.R.V. No. 1276, at the then-terminal of the "J" rail line between Church and Dolores Streets. Note the car's red-painted coupler-- a special application of color to designate that a test of modified coupler components was underway on this day, August 21, 1983.

●

CARBARN PRESS®
P.O. BOX 1990
ORANGEVALE, CA 95662-1990

TABLE OF CONTENTS

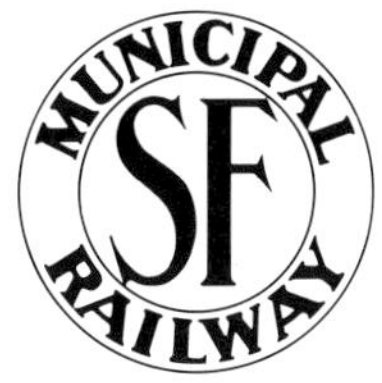

FOREWORD..4

INTRODUCTION..5

1.............................LIGHT RAIL DIVISION 6

2.............................CABLE CAR DIVISION 22

3.............................TROLLEY COACHES 30

4.............................MOTOR COACHES...................................36

5.............................MUNI PEOPLE...40

6.............................THE TROLLEY FESTIVAL 42

ACKNOWLEDGEMENTS 64

FOREWORD

What began as a temporary 90-day job in August 1969, finally ended nearly 21 years later, on June 11, 1990, when I officially retired from my shopman's position with the San Francisco Municipal Railway. Those years were filled with fun and adventure for this life-long transportation enthusiast, and will always be considered as being among the most memorable experiences of my life.

Where else but in San Francisco could one have gripped cable cars, run vintage and modern streetcars, operated old and new trolley coaches, and driven a variety of diesel buses? I was able to do all of those things, as well as learn the requirements of keeping those same vehicles repaired and serviceable. My work sites have included almost all Muni maintenance facilities, at one time or other, through a variety of job assignments.

For all of those years I usually carried my camera to work with me....for who could tell what unusual event would be available to immortalize on film? Therefore, many of the views presented in this album were available only to Municipal Railway employees, or were posed especially by me or by my fellow workers for the purpose of being photographed.

If you, the reading public, create a demand, there will be other Muni color albums in the future, for the transparencies reproduced here are but a small sampling of the many images that I was able to capture during my Muni career. Therefore, let us hope that we will meet again in future volumes, to review photographically the exciting operations of the San Francisco Municipal Railway.

Fair Oaks, California
June 1991

Jeffrey Moreau

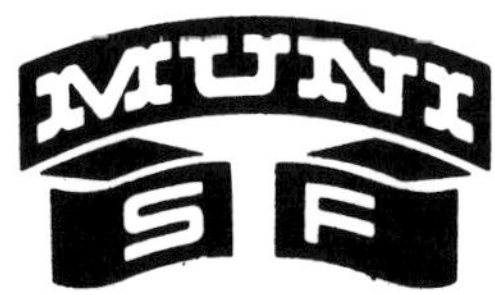

INTRODUCTION

Thanks to an enlightened population dwelling in the United States of America, and its influence upon local and federal legislators, a notable renewing and constructing of mass transportation systems within America's largest cities and urban population centers was undertaken in the late 1960's and continued throughout the 1970's. Although the pace of those halcyon years has slowed considerably in recent times due to political pressures from petroleum and automotive interests, the rebuilding and expanding of the country's public transit services continues as our streets and highways become clogged with vehicular traffic and begin more to resemble parking lots than traffic thoroughfares.

The city of San Francisco was among the first of several large American cities to take advantage of the federal government's financial largesse towards the upgrading of existing urban transit systems. During the years 1967-1991, the San Francisco Municipal Railway has been able to completely replace its electric rail, electric bus, and diesel coach fleets through matching-funds grants from the Urban Mass Transportation Administration of the United States government. In addition, other Muni projects funded jointly with U.M.T.A. were the complete replacement of old electro-mechanical power substations with up-to-the-minute solid-state equipment; the complete rebuilding of the Muni power distribution system; the re-railing of most trackage on the city's five streetcar routes; replacement of the entire fixed plant and power station of the cable railway lines with brand-new structures and components; two new extentions to the streetcar network; conversion of two major diesel bus lines to trolley coach services; shifting operations of the five Muni streetcar lines off the city's main thoroughfare, Market Street, into the B.A.R.T.D.-owned, Muni-operated, Market Street streetcar subway; installation of a modern radio communications system; construction of the new Woods motor coach operating and rebuilding center; construction of a new carpenter shop and cable car rebuilding facility; construction of the new streetcar storage yard and major overhaul shops at the Green Division; construction of a new office building housing various Muni departments at San Jose and Geneva Avenues; and the complete replacement of the old Geneva carbarn with a new running repair and maintenance building, together with an upgraded storage yard.

Although the previous paragraph has listed most of the major undertakings that have been completed by the San Francisco Municipal Railway during the past 25 years, many additional, albeit smaller, projects were undertaken simultaneously. Prior to this recent time period, the Muni had remained a system virtually unchanged since the integration and modernization of the former Market Street Railway Company lines and facilities after their purchase by the city on September 29, 1944.

For followers of urban transit operations, the next few years should prove to be equally exciting in the City By The Bay; promised are a new streetcar line utilizing rebuilt P.C.C.—type cars over almost the entire length of Market Street, as well as new electric railway trackage along most of the northern waterfront. This is being done in conjunction with a new parkway project coming in the wake of the removal of the ill-fated Embarcadero Freeway, due to that roadway's extensive damage from the October 17, 1989, Loma Prieta earthquake. Additionally, the upcoming years promise the extension of Muni Metro service to the new Mission Bay business/residential development, conversion of additional diesel bus lines to electric coach operations, new light rail cars, new articulated trolley coaches, and operation of the railway's historic streetcar fleet on a full-time basis.

Let us then return, for the time being, to the recent past to view the Municipal Railway as it undergoes a metamorphosis from a 1950's-era transit system into a 1990's high-technology urban transportation entity.

1

LIGHT RAIL DIVISION

San Francisco, unlike a majority of American cities that had abandoned their electrically-powered streetcar lines and replaced those services with rubber-tired vehicles in the 1940's and 1950's, chose to retain five well-patronized streetcar lines as the major core routes of its comprehensive city-wide transit system. Chief among the reasons for retention of those lines were the existance of two lengthy tunnels constructed years before for exclusive use by streetcars to bypass formidable grades on the hills that those tunnels were bored through. (The long Twin Peaks Tunnel, with a heavily-used underground station, is utilized by the "K", "L", and "M" lines, while the shorter Sunset Tunnel is traversed by the "N" line.)

As a side benefit to the passage of the 1962 bond measure allowing construction of the Bay Area Rapid Transit District's heavy-rail mass transit system, the people of San Francisco were to be provided with a separate subway tunnel under their city's Market Street for use by a to-be-determined electric railway transit line. After many changes of plan, city officials finally decided to utilize the new Market Street subway in conjunction with the operation of the five existing Municipal Railway streetcar lines.

The story of the immense amount of work done to transform and link-up those five San Francisco electric railway lines with the underground bore constructed beneath Market Street in the late 1960's, would fill an entire volume of its own; however, the reader can well imagine the vast amount of construction activity that took place while most of the rail, overhead, power distribution system, and power substations, were completely rebuilt to the standards required by a modern light rail transit operation. Included in the upgrading of the system was the design, and construction, of a new fleet of electric streetcars able to provide both low-level, street loading of passengers, as well as high-platform loading capabilities.

Moreover, two extentions of the Municipal Railway streetcar system have been made in order to give additional flexibility to Muni's light rail operations. The outer end of line "M", through new trackage constructed on Broad Street and San Jose Avenue, was linked-up in 1980 to the outer end of line "K" adjacent to the Balboa Park B.A.R.T.D. station; in early 1991, a major new track extention to line "J" was completed, linking up that route to line "K" near the same Balboa Park B.A.R.T.D. station.

Though ridership upon the five Municipal Railway streetcar lines has increased dramatically in the years since operations began in the Muni Metro subway under Market Street, the quality of service has fallen drastically due to problems encountered with having enough of the railway's trouble-plagued light rail vehicles available for revenue service. Since taking delivery of the first of the so-called "United States Standard Light Rail Vehicles" in late 1977, this group of cars has proven itself to be a labor-intensive, easily-disabled fleet of rolling stock. Utilizing its own engineering staff, as well as outside consultants, the Municipal Railway has come up with the design for an entirely-new fleet of light rail vehicles destined to replace the present cars in the mid-1990's; Muni is hoping to be able to award a contract in late 1991, for construction of 50 of these new vehicles in order to help alleviate its chronic car shortage problem. If the new design proves itself a worthy successor after in-service trials, then enough additional vehicles will be purchased to completely retire the Boeing L.R.V. fleet from active duty, and to provide an increase in service frequency for the Municipal Railway's streetcar division.

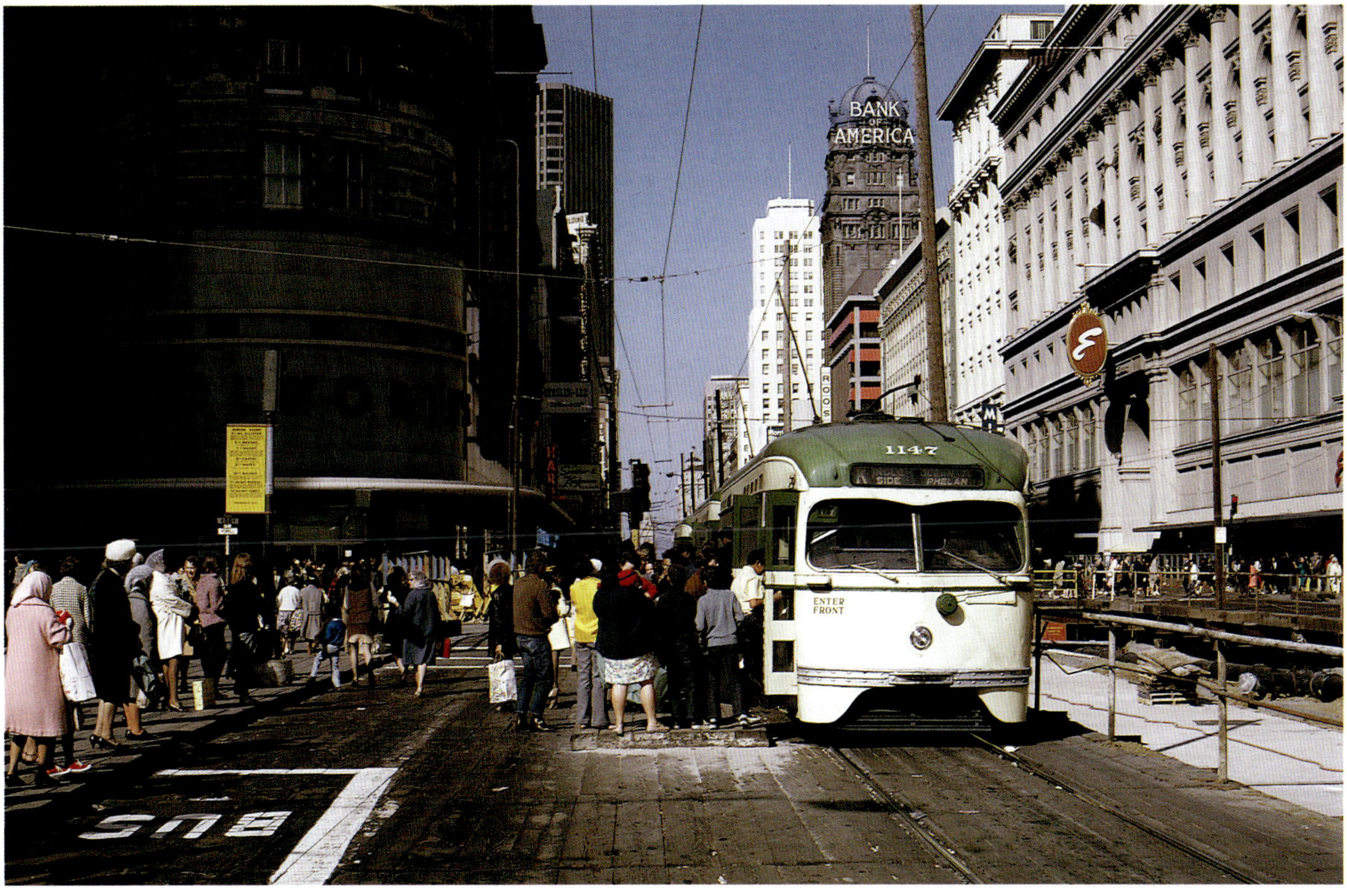

(ABOVE) Looking north along Market Street, at Powell Street, we note car No. 1147 outbound on line "K", in May 1970. Temporary wooden beams are still in place as work continues on the final phases of completing the B.A.R.T.D./Muni Market Street Subway, and the Powell Street underground station.
(BELOW) Stopped at the 8th Street loading platform, outbound along Market Street, car No. 1016 is providing its usual comfortable service for patrons of line "J", in December 1972.

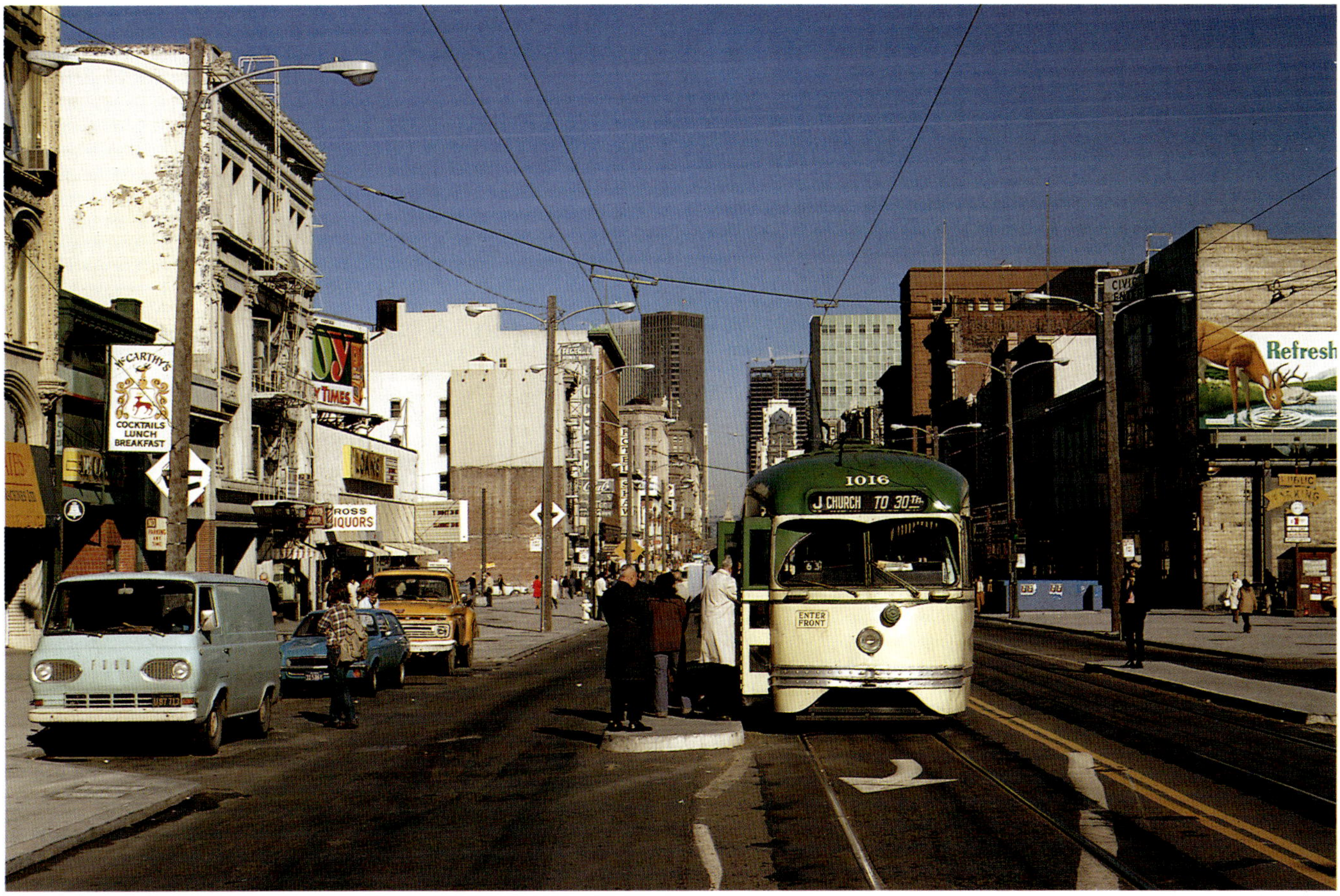

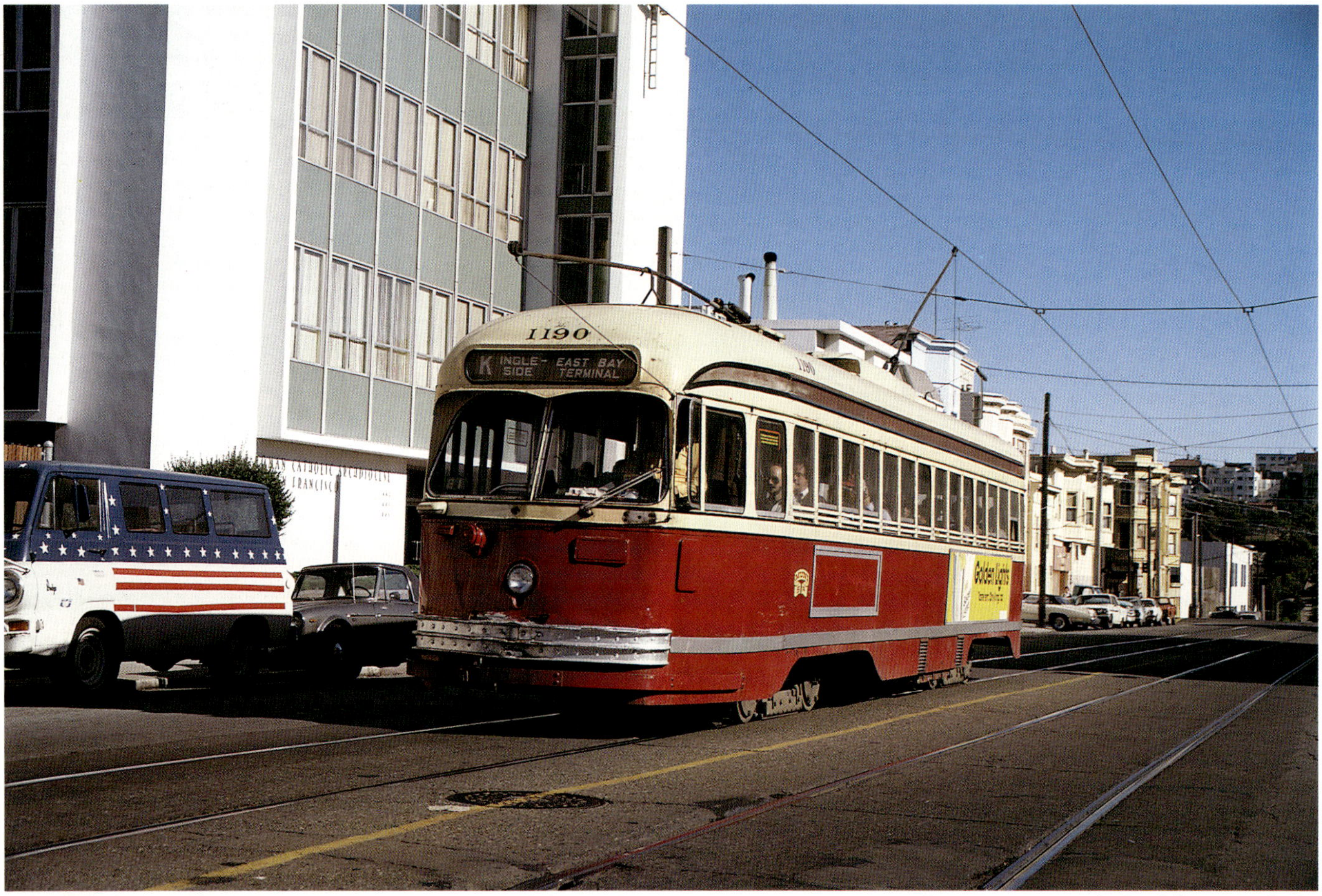

(ABOVE) One of eleven such cars purchased from the Toronto Transportation Commission to help fill extended headways made necessary by the Market Street subway construction project, P.C.C. car No. 1190 heads inbound on Church Street, just north of 17th Street, on July 30, 1979. These cars, highly unreliable, mechanically speaking, were a short-lived Muni phenomenon.

(BELOW) Former passenger car No. 1008 was converted into the Metro Division wrecker car and given the exotic paint scheme it wears as it proceeds west along Ulloa Street, on line "L" trackage, on May 20, 1981.

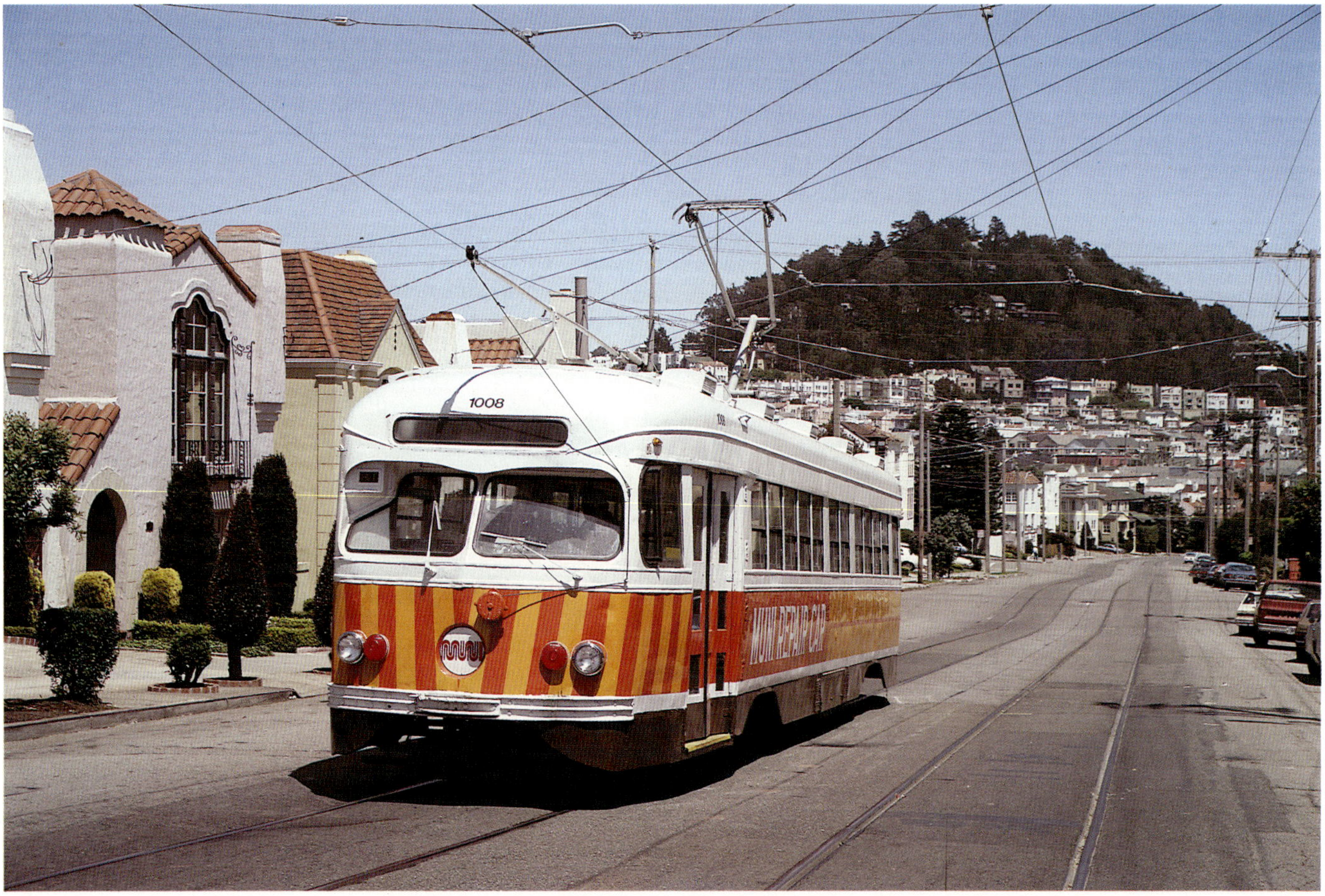

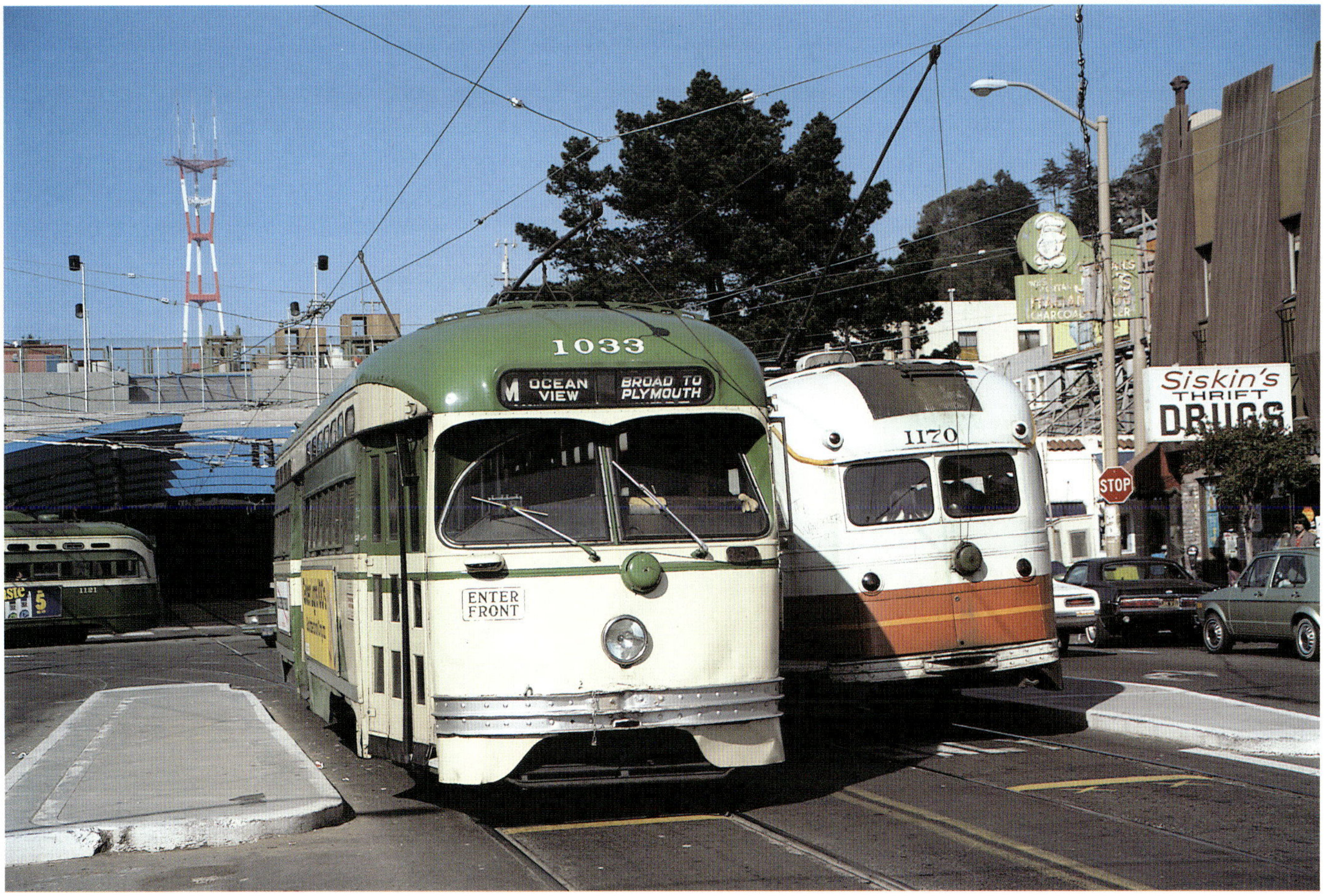

(ABOVE) After construction of the new West Portal high-level station, temporary low-level loading platforms were installed for use by P.C.C. cars still in use on lines "K", "L", and "M". Here, car No. 1033 is shown leaving one of the temporary platforms, located on West Portal Avenue, in April 1979.
(BELOW) Taken in approximately the same location as the lower photo of the preceeding page, we are looking east along Ulloa Street from 15th Avenue, on April 4, 1981. Car No. 1, Muni's first streetcar, is photographed while on a private charter over the city's various electrified street railway lines. That's scenic Mt. Davidson in the background.

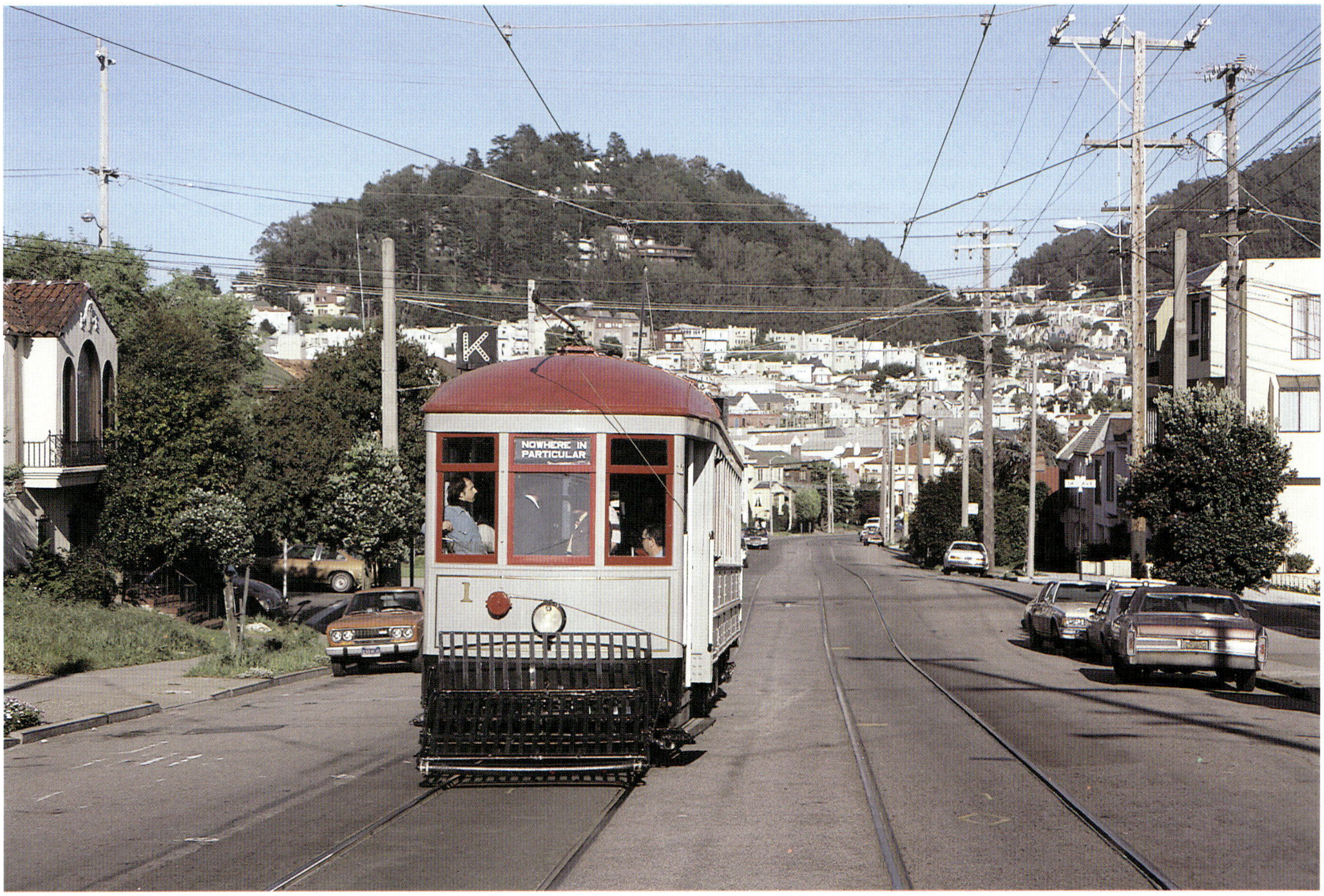

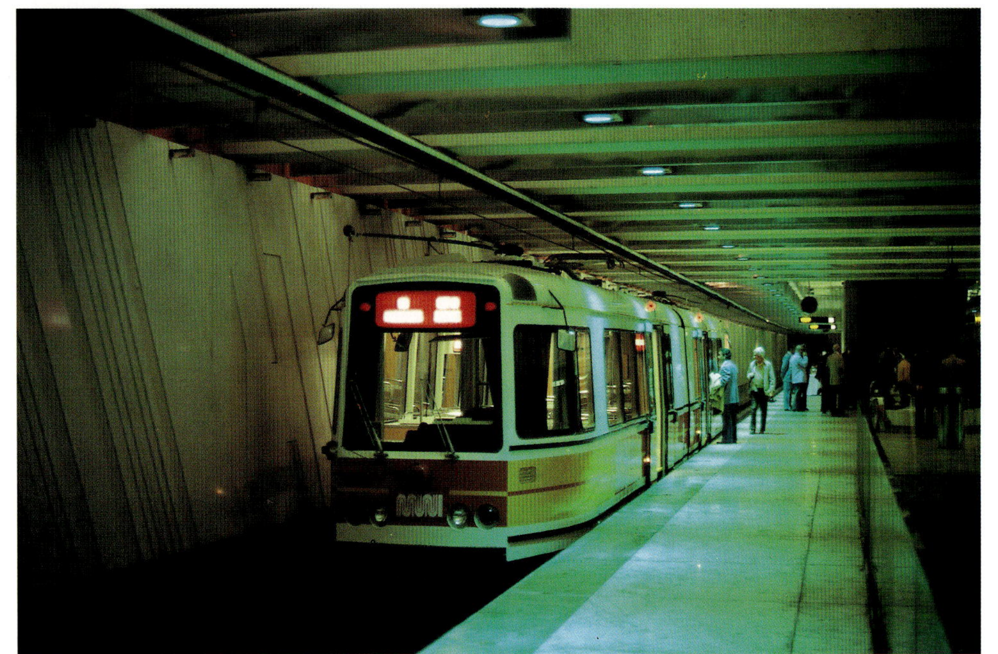

Here we are at the press preview of the Municipal Railway's new Market Street Subway, held at the Embarcadero Station on January 31, 1978. Car No. 1220(I) is awaiting its load of invited passengers, as Muni's genial official photographer, Marshall Moxom, hurries to board the car in advance of the assembled guests.

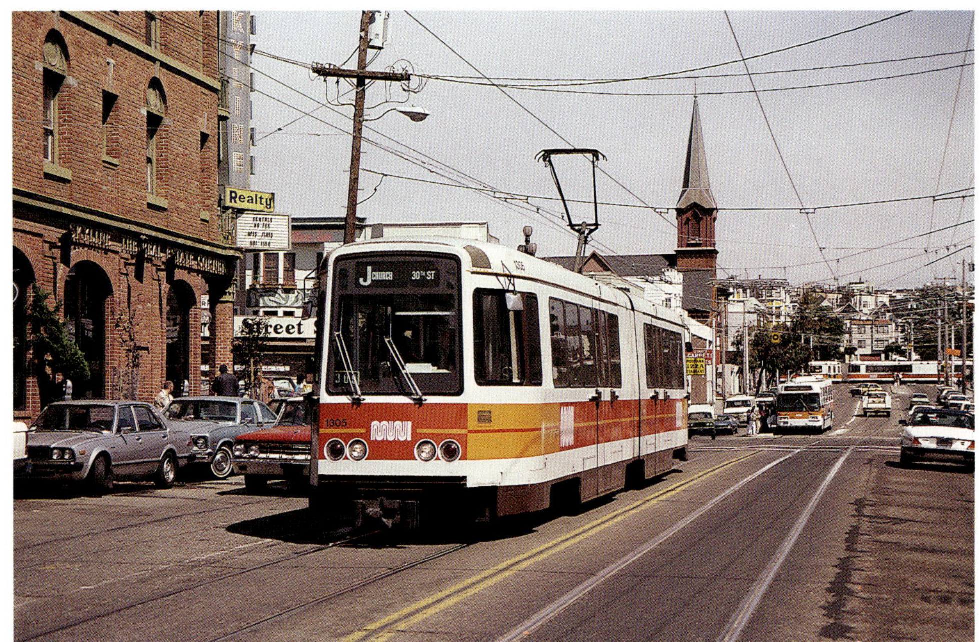

L.R.V. No. 1305, one of 30 cars purchased by Muni from manufacturer Boeing after being rejected by Boston's transit agency, is seen southbound at Church and Market Streets, on Line "J", in August 1984.

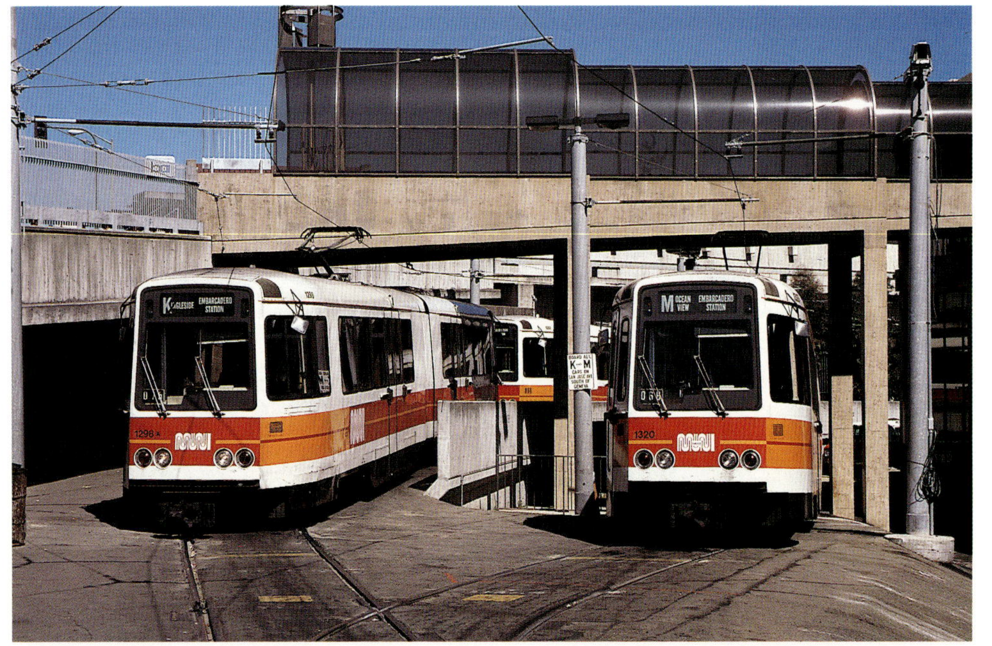

For a brief period of time, line "M" shared the Balboa Park terminal facilities with line "K"-- as seen in this view taken on May 22, 1985. However, service delays encountered on the off-street revenue loop caused the transfer of line "M" trains to a loop operation within Geneva Yard, just across the street from the previous terminal.

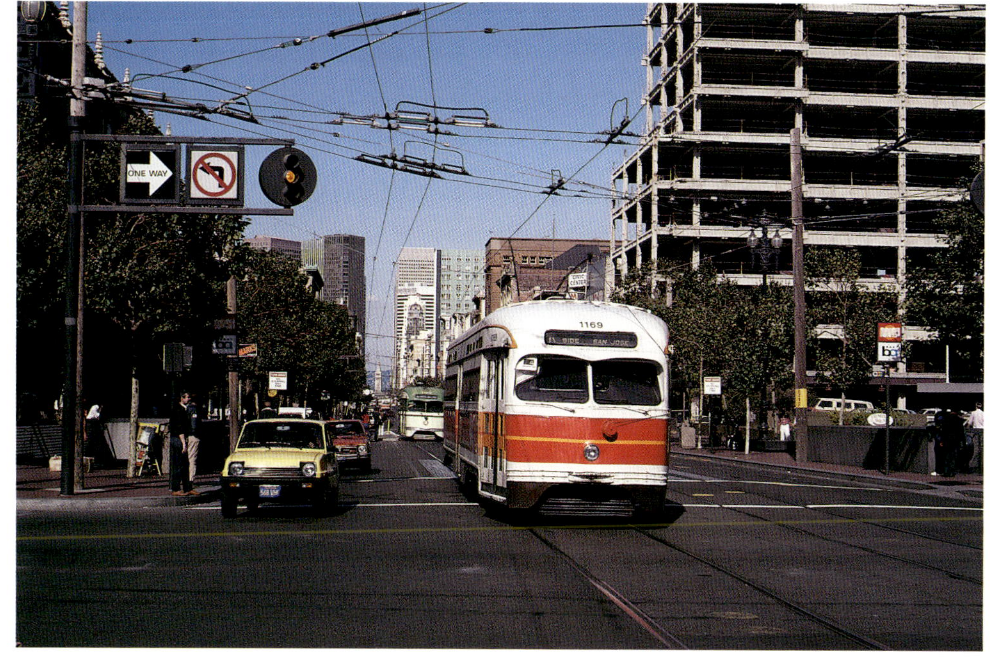

During the last months of surface operations for line "K", we note car No. 1169 outbound on Market Street, at 8th Street, on September 19, 1982.

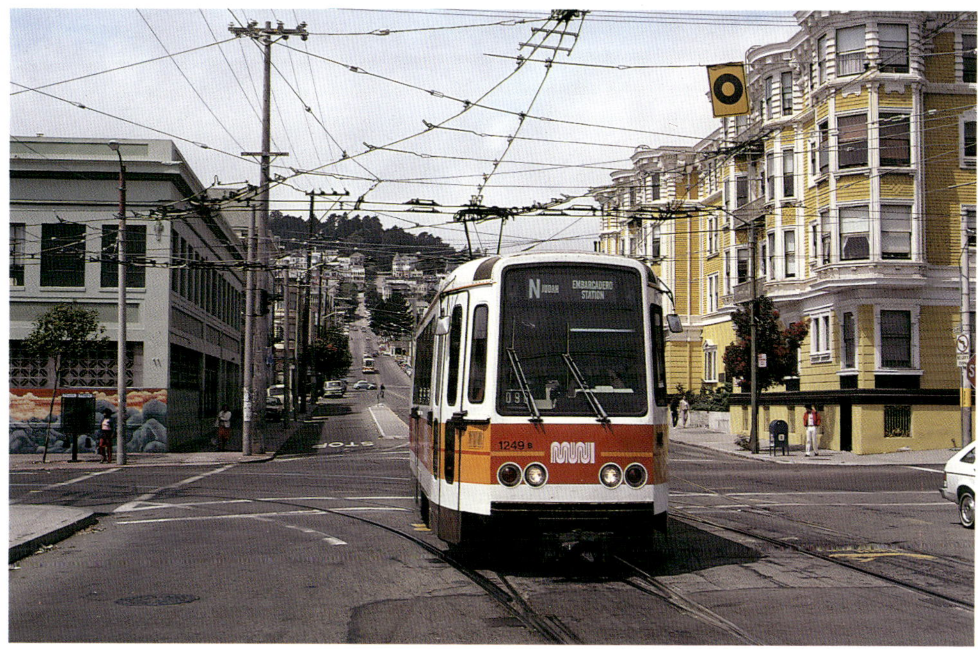

Line "N" was the first streetcar line converted to full-time L.R.V. operation, and the first streetcar line to operate in the new Market Street Subway. Here, car No. 1249 heads eastbound across Church Street, from Duboce Avenue, toward the entrance ramp of the Muni Metro Subway on August 19, 1982.

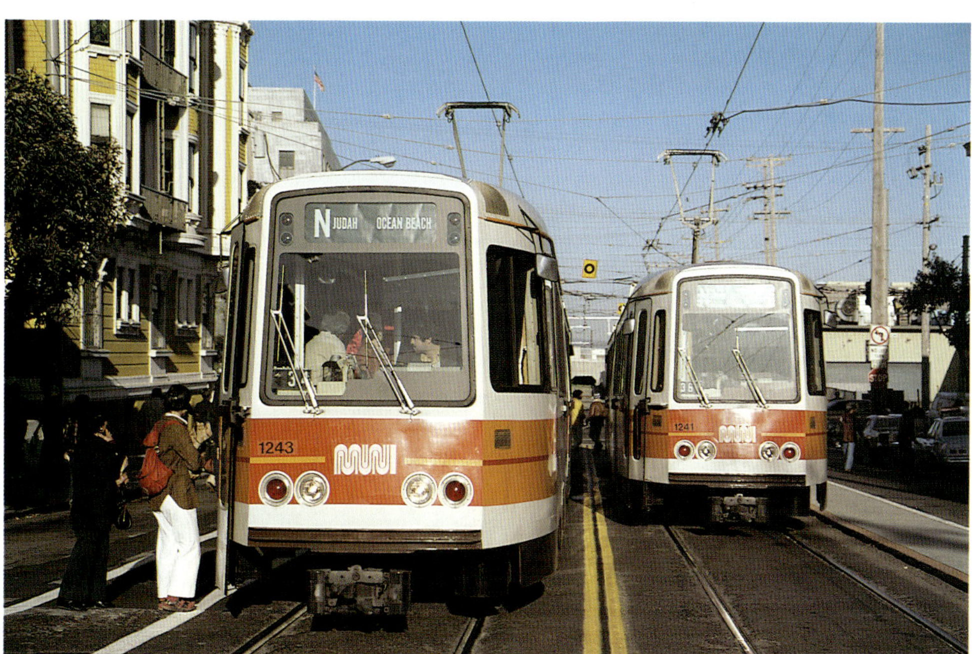

Rush hour on line "N"-- here are two trains loading passengers at the Duboce Avenue platforms, just west of Church Street, on the afternoon of April 1, 1980.

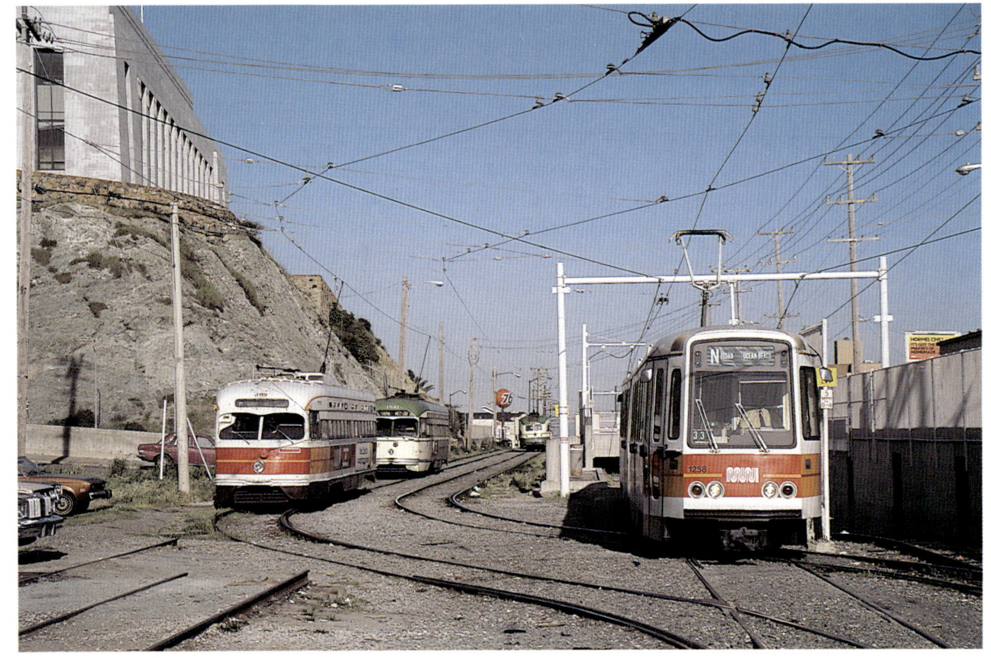

Line "K" and line "L" P.C.C. cars await their turn to enter the west junction on the Duboce Avenue private-right-of-way, as Line "N" L.R.V. No. 1258 heads west on April 1, 1980.

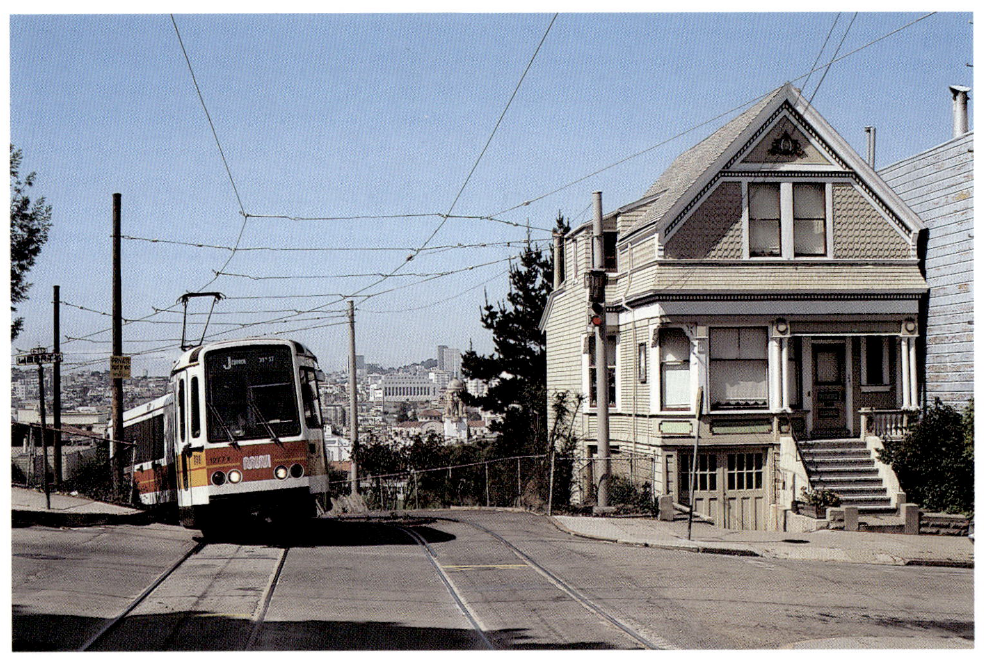

Passing one of San Francisco's classic Victorian-era buildings, line "J" L.R.V. No. 1277 crosses Liberty Street, outbound, on August 12, 1982.

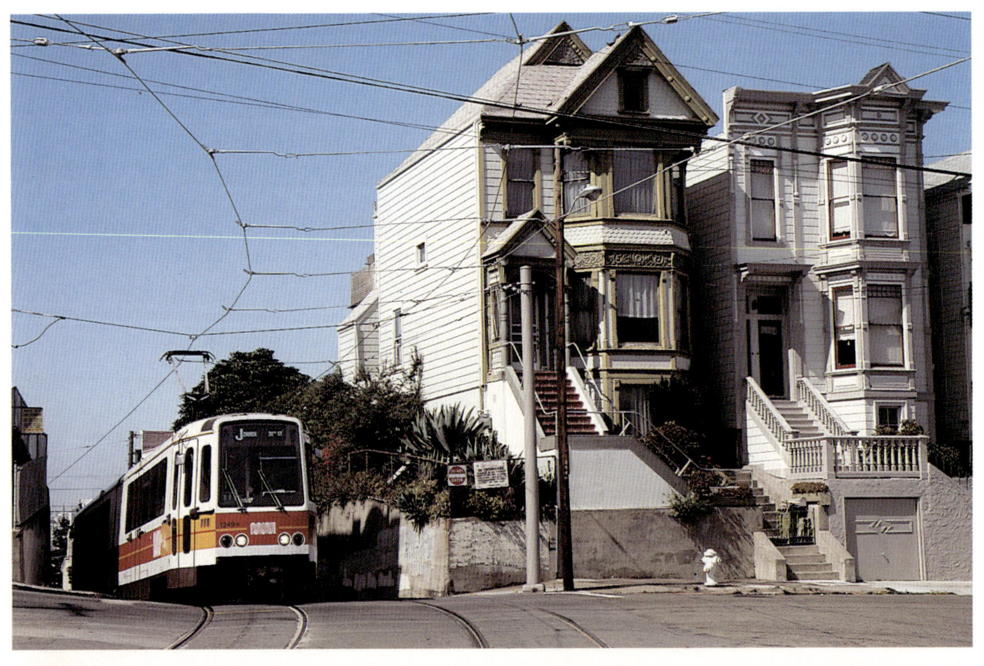

Just south of Liberty Street, line "J crosses 21st Street amid another cluster of beautiful homes. Here, car No. 1249 crests the P.R./W. at 21st Street on August 12, 1982.

Initial L.R.V. revenue service was a shuttle operation on line "K", between West Portal Station and the Balboa Park B.A.R.T.D. station. Car No. 1238, shown on Ulloa Street at Lenox Way, in May 1979, was one of the first of the new cars to enter service.

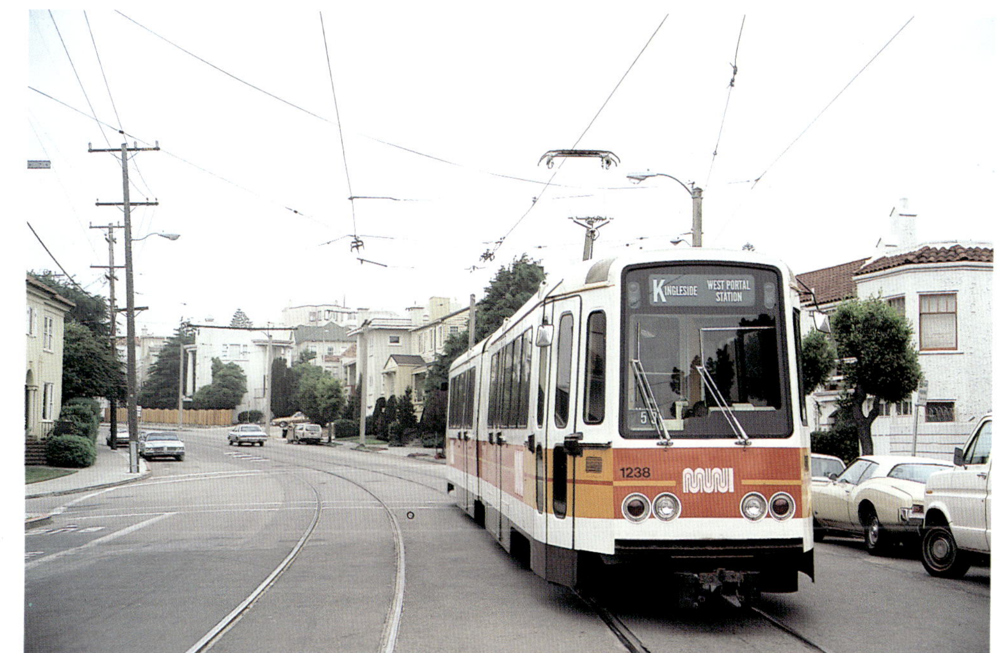

Southbound at St. Francis Circle in June 1979, car No. 1234, on line "K", offers the promise of a new standard of travel for local residents.

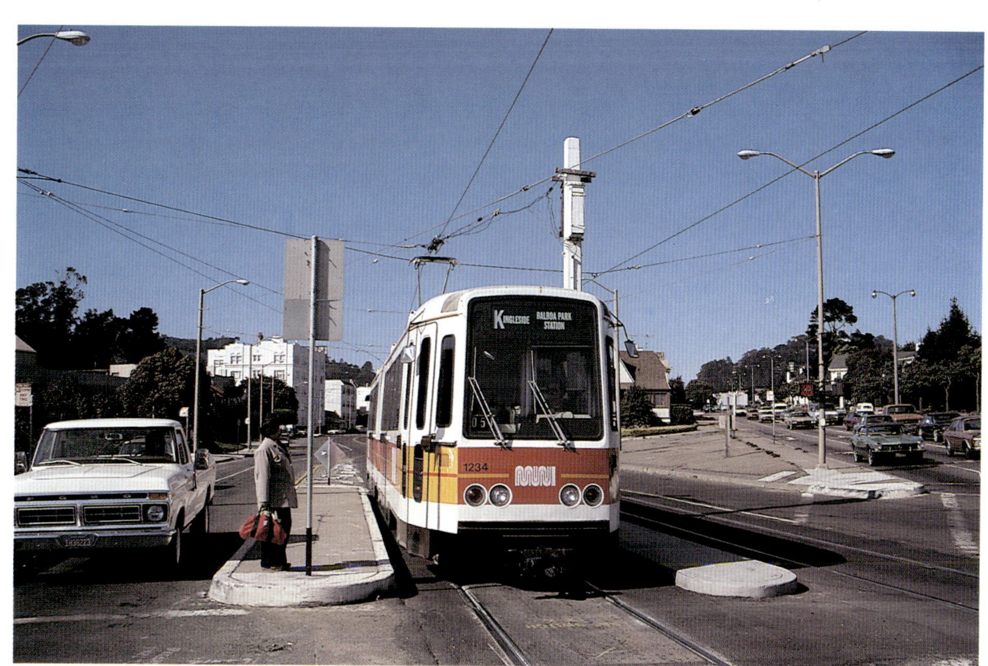

An outbound line "K" streetcar, No. 1277, has just unloaded a passenger at the Victoria Street traffic island, and proceeds east along Ocean Avenue on March 15, 1988.

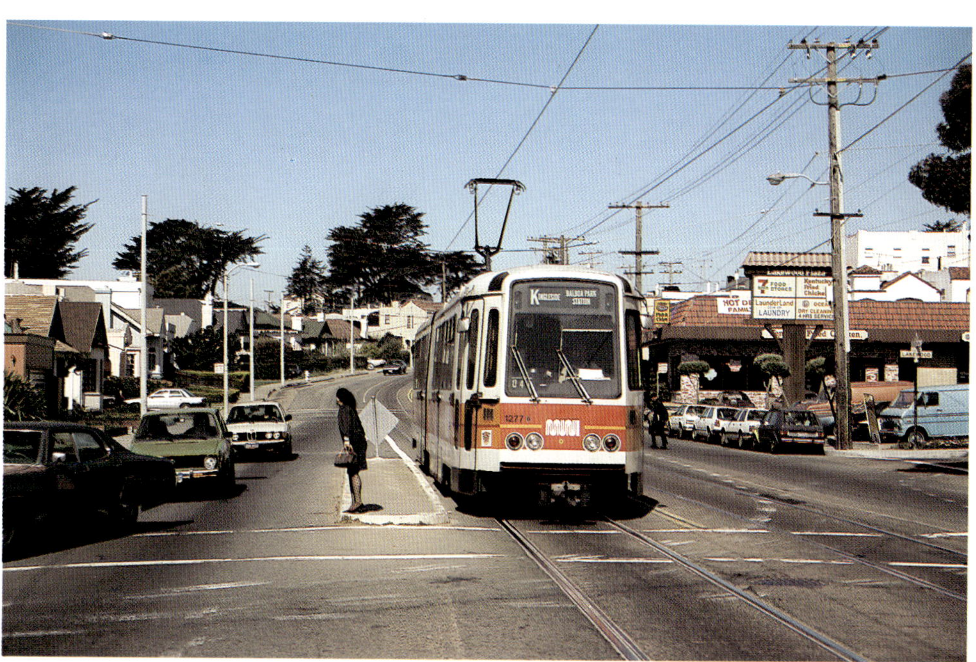

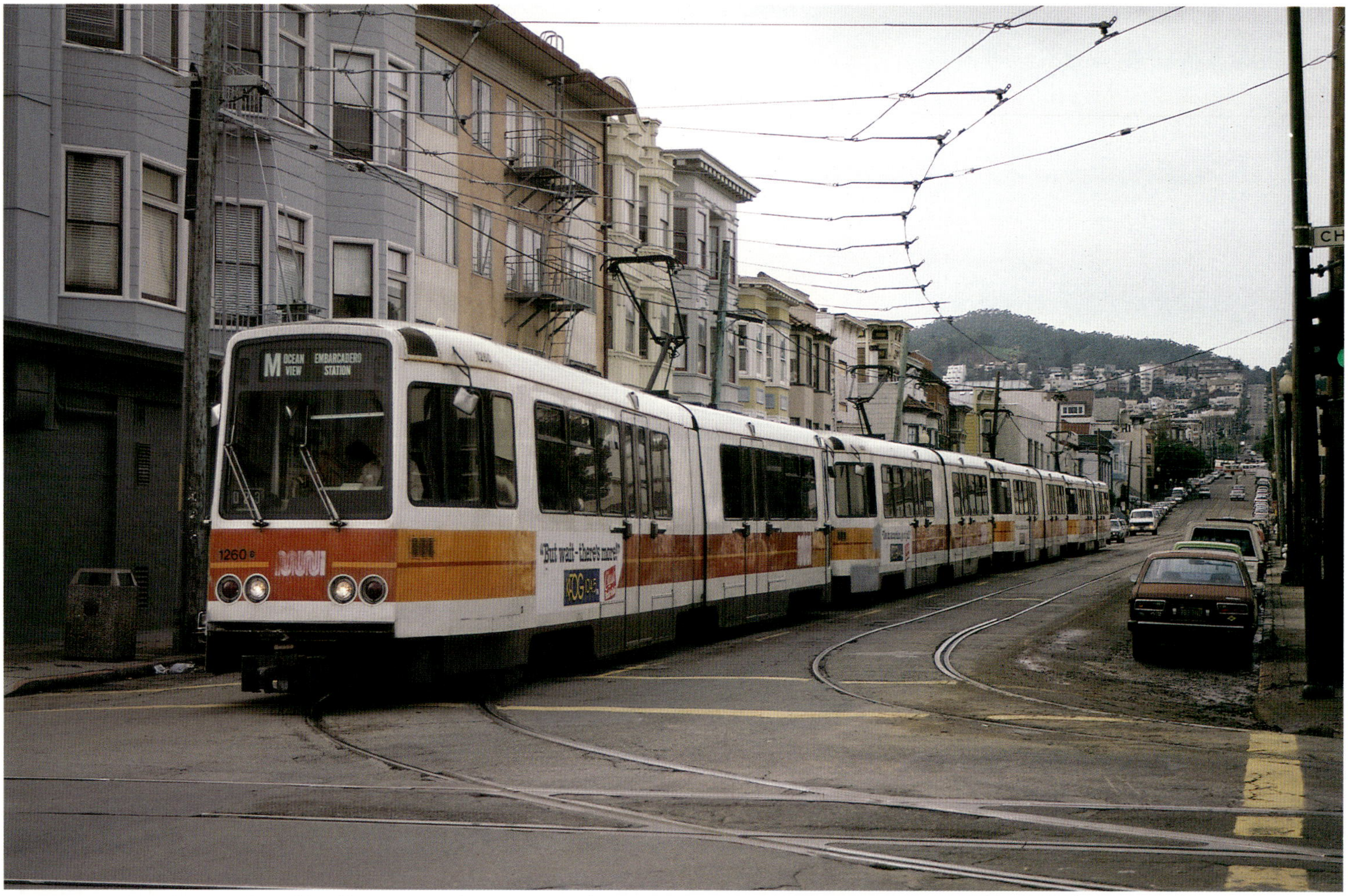

(ABOVE) After the overhead had been rebuilt to accomodate pantograph operation, Muni was able to utilize its trackage on 17th Street, between Church and Castro Streets, as an alternate route during emergencies in the Market Street Subway. One such occurance, the flooding of the Church Street Station after a heavy rainstorm, caused the 17th Street trackage to be pressed into service on December 8, 1987. Here, car No. 1260 leads a four-car train eastbound along 17th Street as it heads toward the Duboce entrance of the Market Street Subway.
(BELOW) Looking east along 17th Street, from Castro Street, on the same day, we note car No. 1246 leading another four-car train to the Collingwood Street entrance of the Twin Peaks Tunnel.

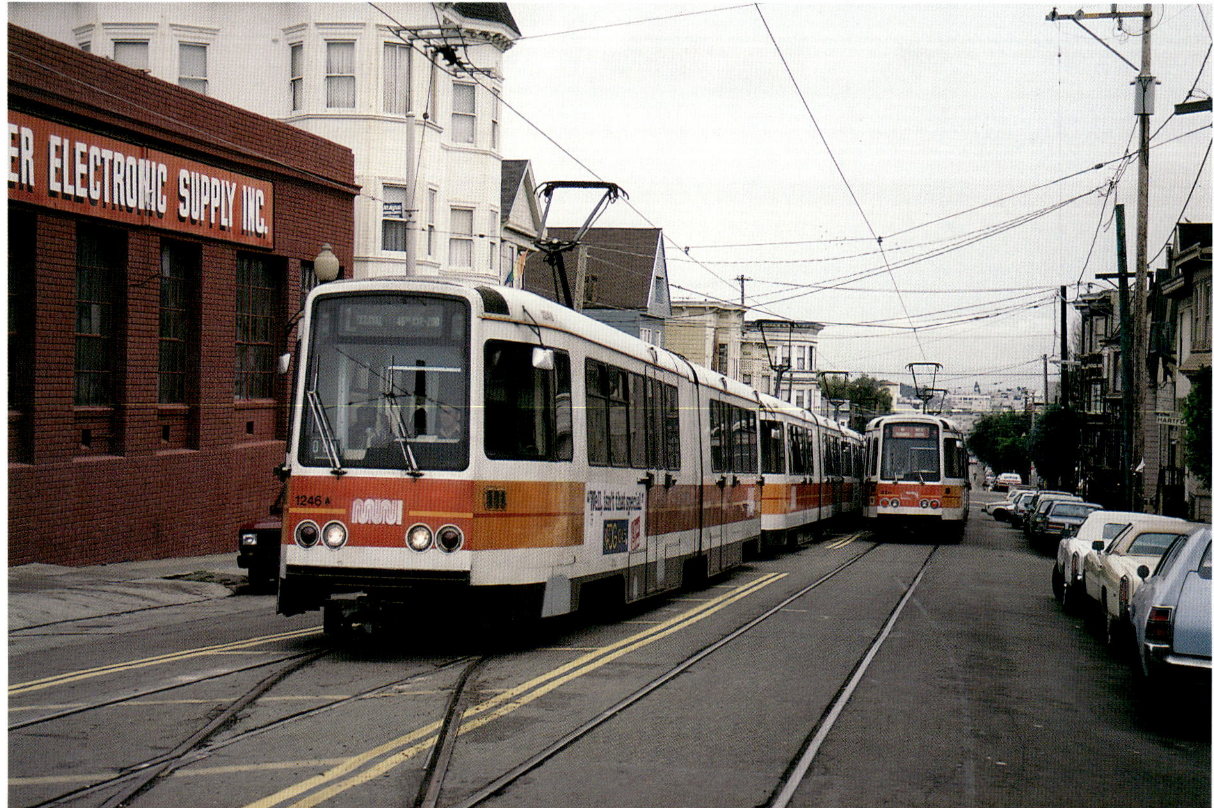

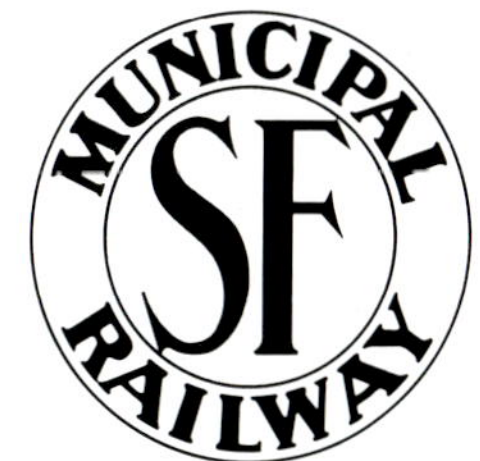

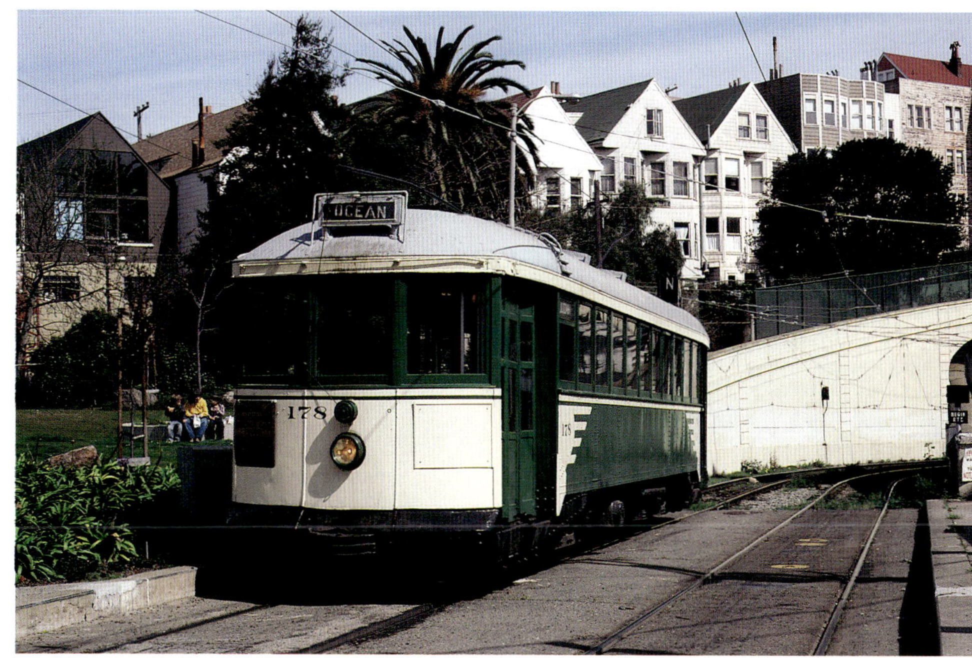

On March 13, 1982, your author sponsored a private excursion aboard vintage car No. 178, on loan to Muni by the Bay Area Electric Railroad Association. Here that vehicle is seen just past the western end of line "N"'s Sunset Tunnel.

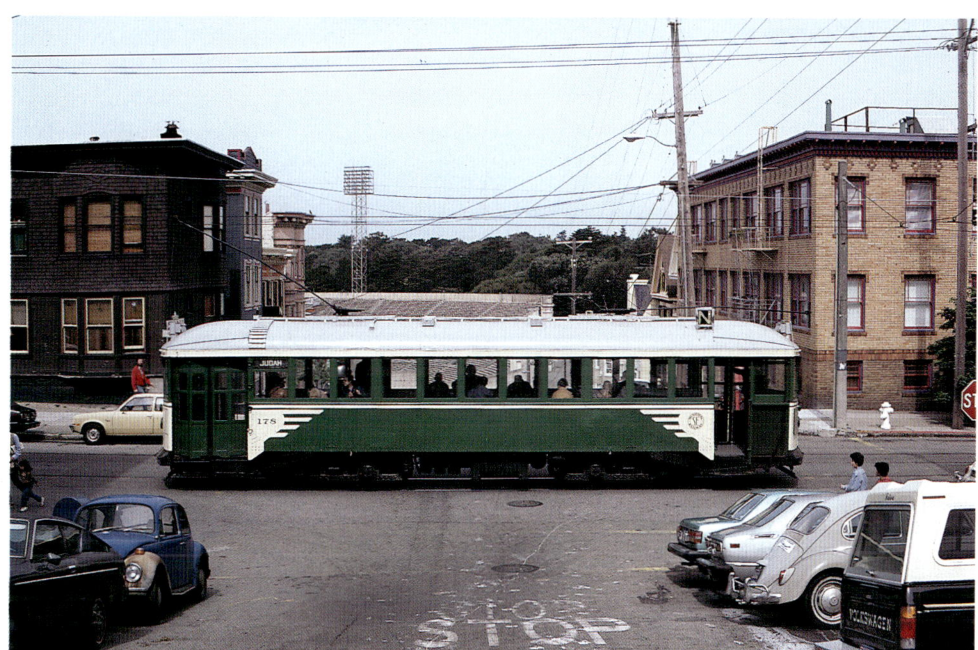

Inbound on line "N", traversing Carl Street, car No. 178 paused at Willard Street to allow a photograph to be taken with the now-demolished Kezar Stadium in the background.

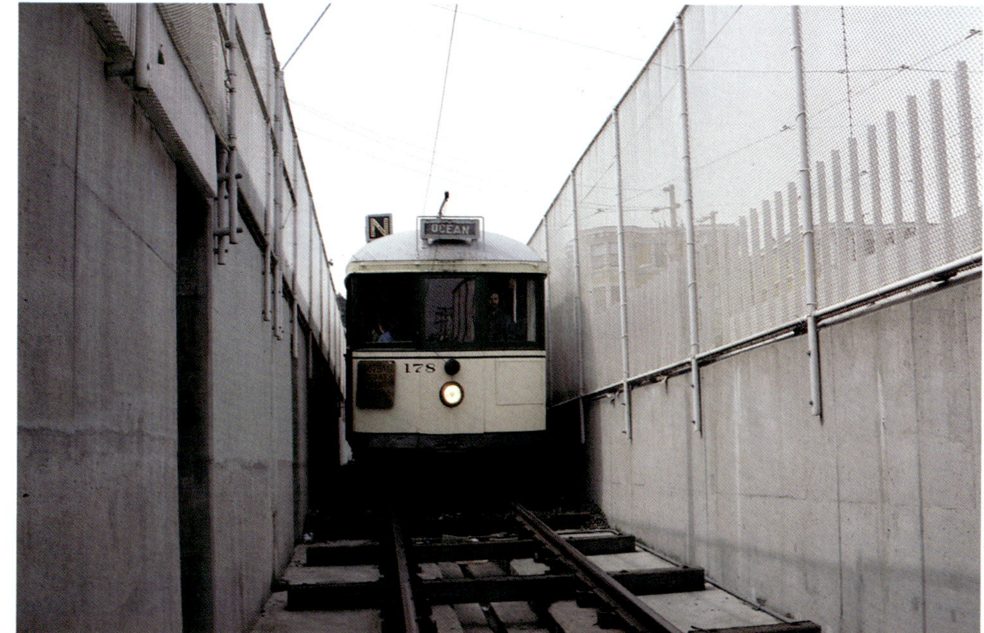

We wanted to be the first of Muni's vintage streetcars into the new Market Street Subway, but this was as far as we were able to travel that day. Car No. 178 is on the inbound ramp of line "N"'s subway entrance, just east of Church Street.

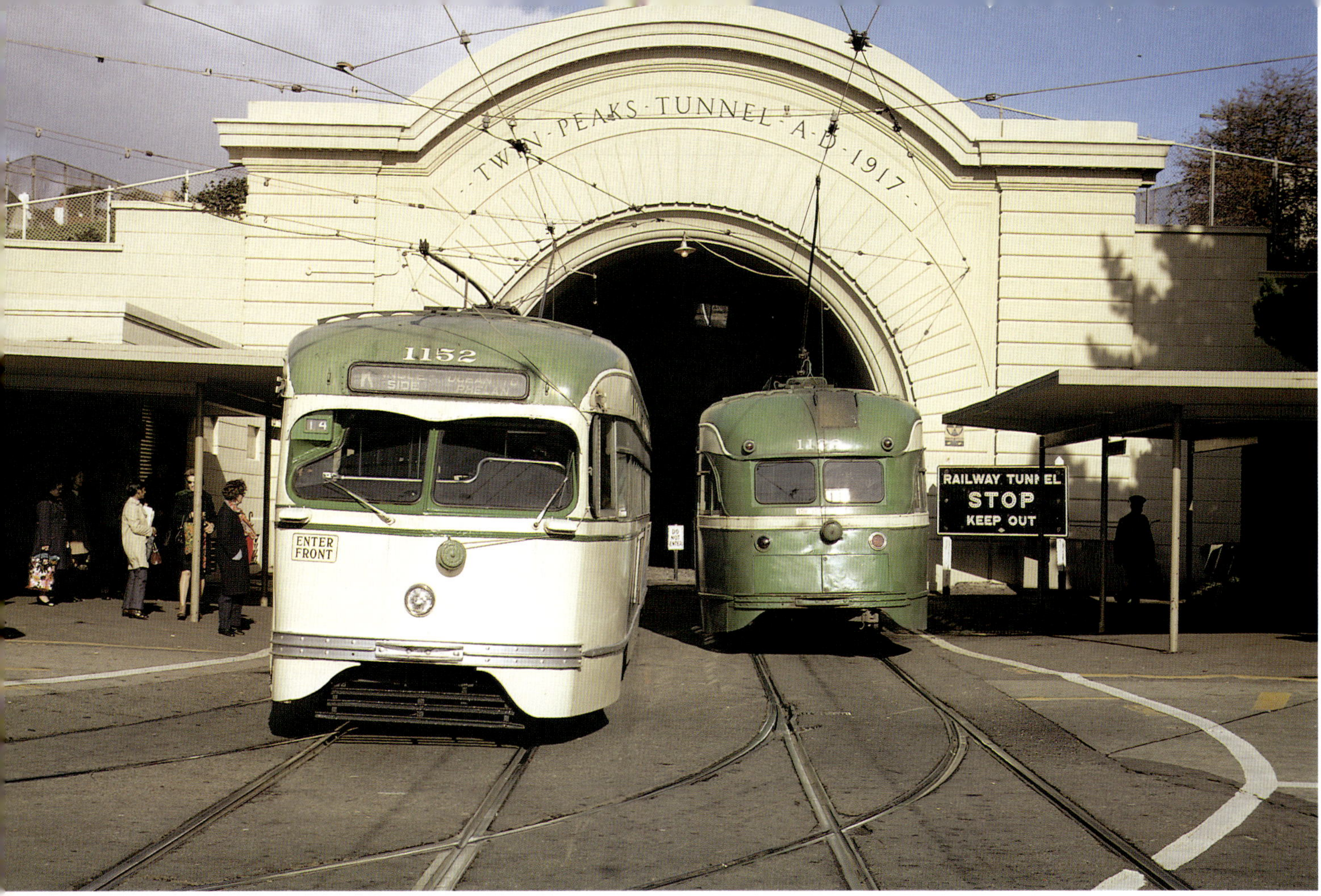

(ABOVE) One of the Muni landmarks most drastically changed during the system's conversion to a modern light rail transit operation was the west portal of the Twin Peaks Tunnel. Here we view the way that that locale had appeared since its construction in 1918, with car No. 1152 on line "K" headed outbound in December 1971.
(BELOW) The present appearance of West Portal Station, now a high-platform facility, shows another outbound line "K" rail car, this time car No. 1227 and train, on December 6, 1980

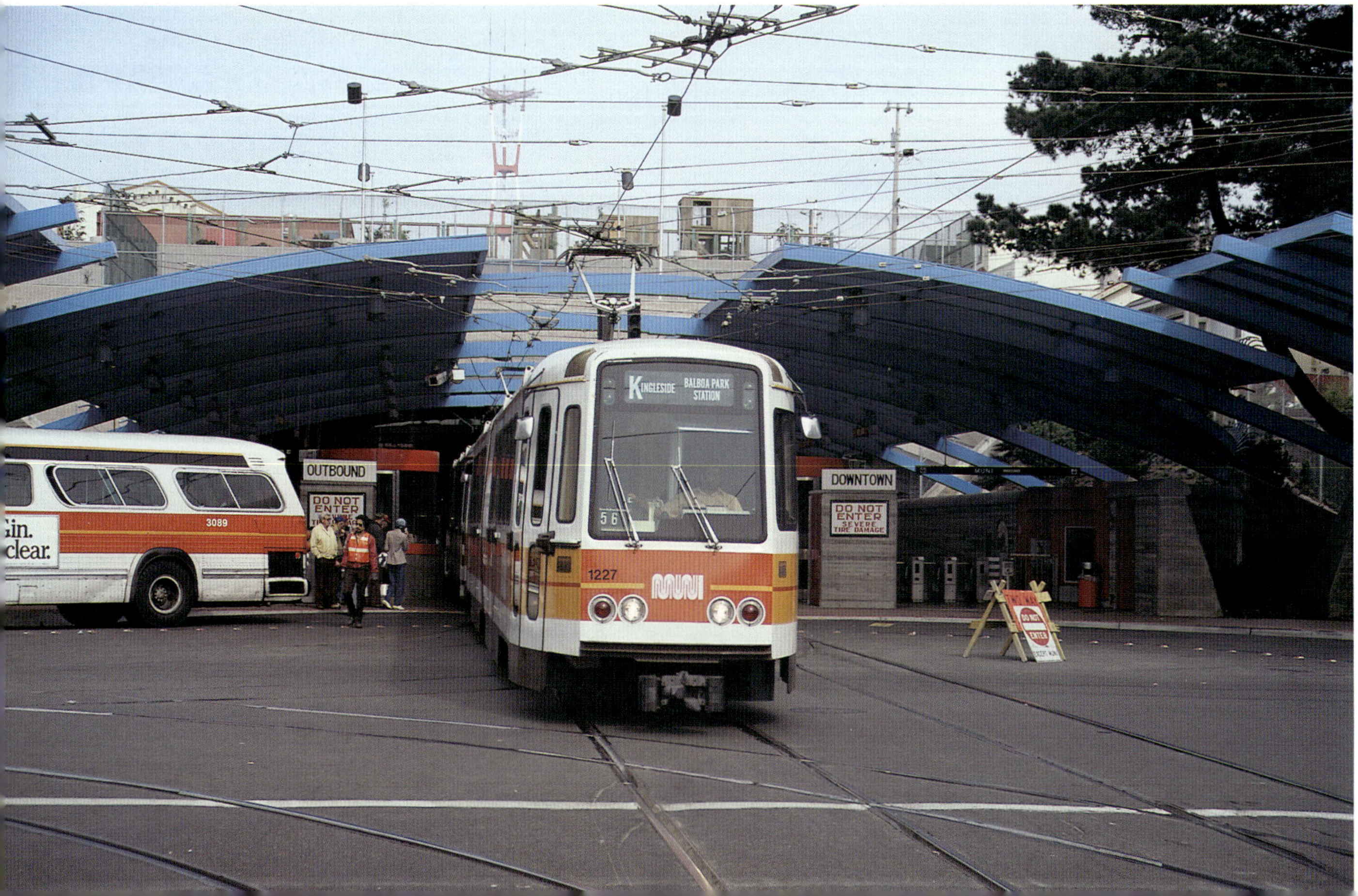

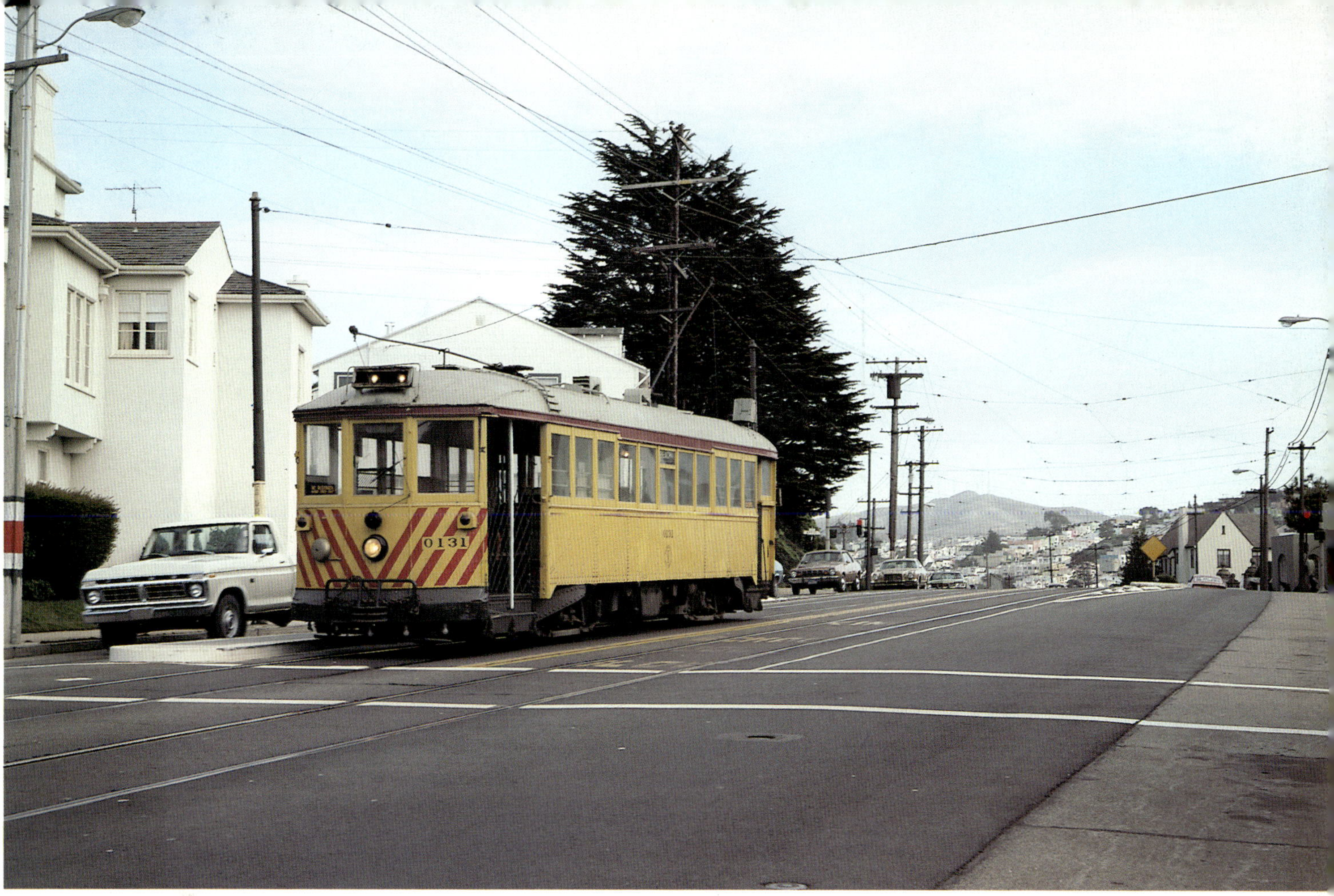

(ABOVE) One Sunday in March 1976, while on duty at Geneva Carbarn with my fellow worker Charlie Camilleri, a call was received from Central Control asking us to retrieve a dead car from the 11th Street spur. Enroute inbound on line "K", we stopped just long enough at San Benito Way to record this view of wrecker No. 0131 in the great outdoors.
(BELOW) With inoperative car No. 1033 in tow, we were on the last leg of our journey home when we paused on San Jose Avenue to snap the photograph reproduced here.

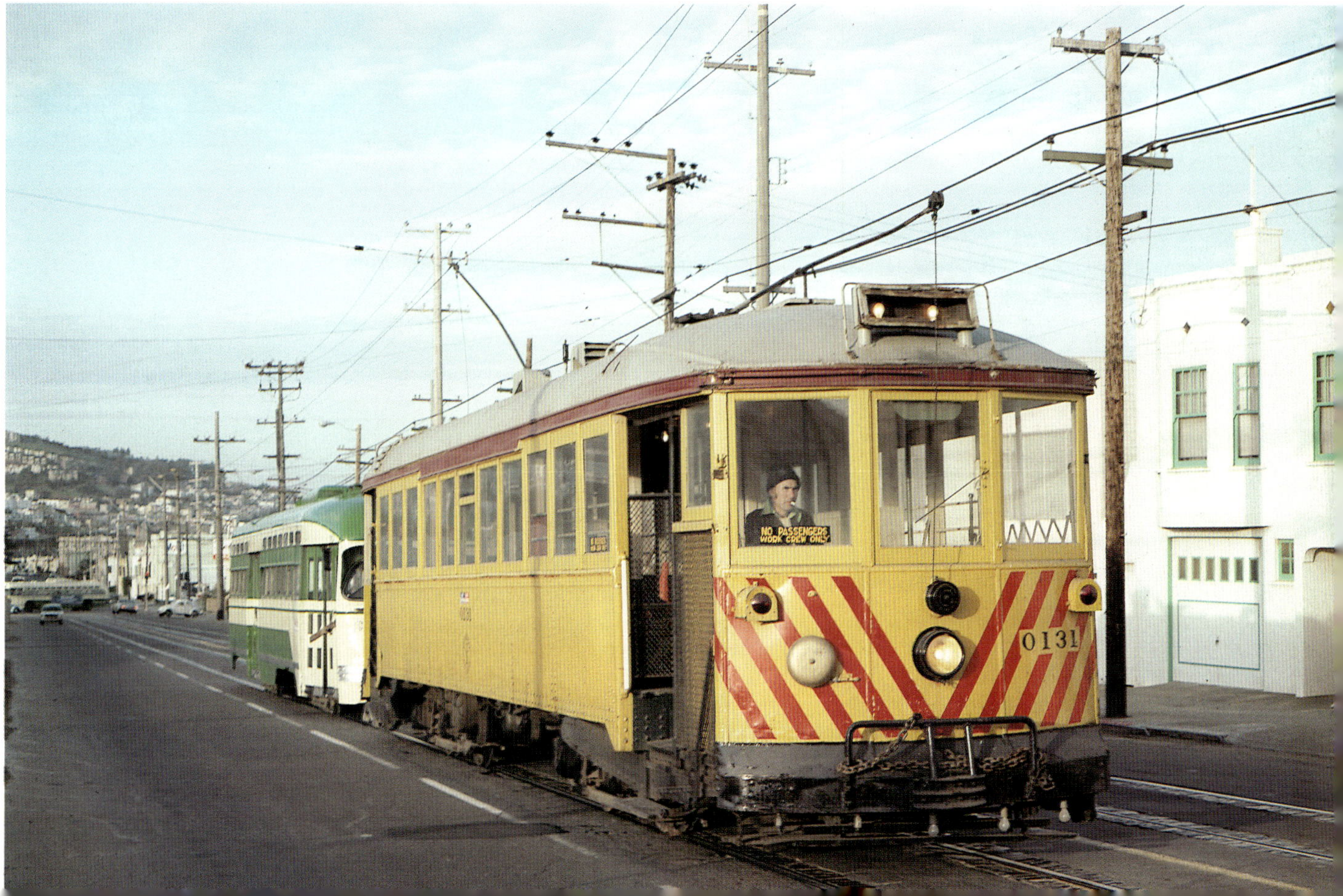

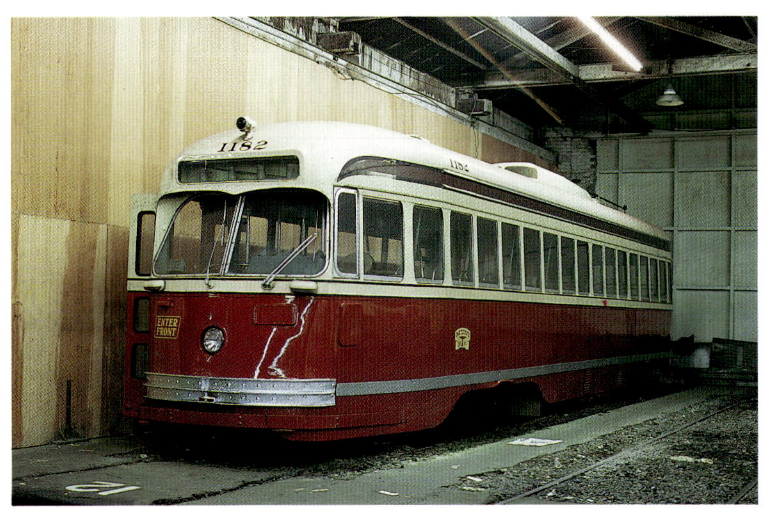

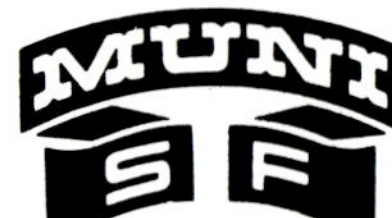

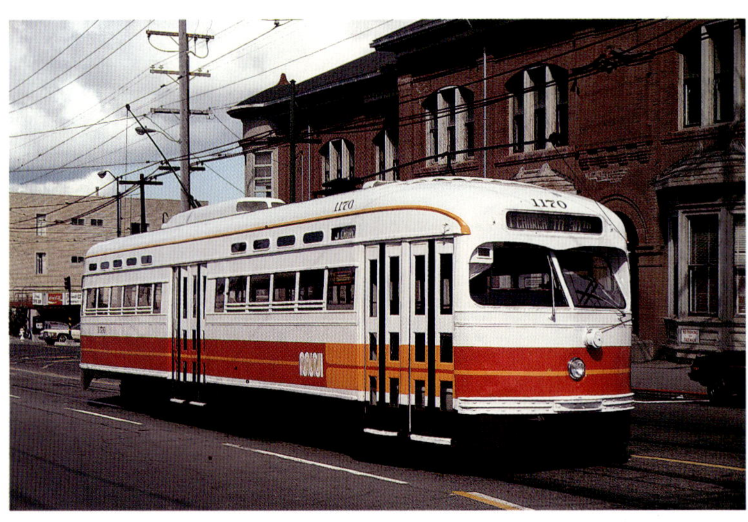

(ABOVE LEFT) Newly-outshopped P.C.C. No. 1182 is shown in Geneva Carbarn after its initial release from Elkton Shops. Note that the car still has its Toronto roof-mounted advance light, and does not yet have a front trolley pole, in this January 1974 photograph.
(ABOVE RIGHT) P.C.C. No. 1170 was Muni's first vehicle painted in the Walter Landor-designed orange/white paint scheme, although the version shown was shortly thereafter modified by increasing the size of the orange bands beneath the windows. The freshly-painted car is posed in front of the Geneva Division office building in April 1977.
(LOWER RIGHT) Only three of Muni's L.R.V.s were equipped with trolley poles, in addition to their standard pantograph; here, car No. 1222, one of that select group, is seen thus equipped in April 1979.
(LOWER LEFT) Trolley pole-equipped car No. 1221(I) is shown at Metro Center Shop shortly after its arrival on Muni property; later returned to Boeing for modifications, this vehicle was renumbered to No. 1213 prior to its second journey to California.

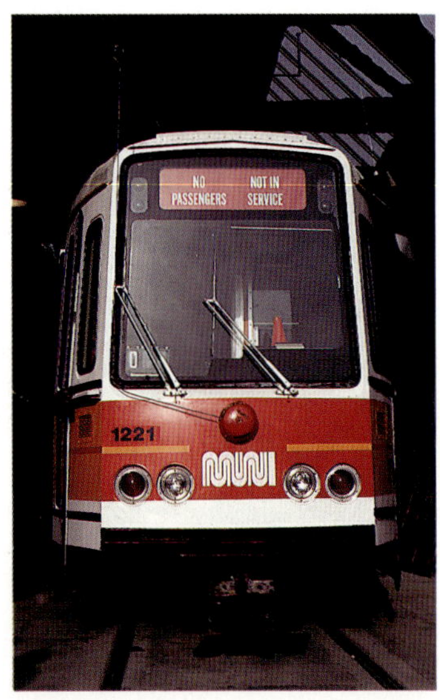

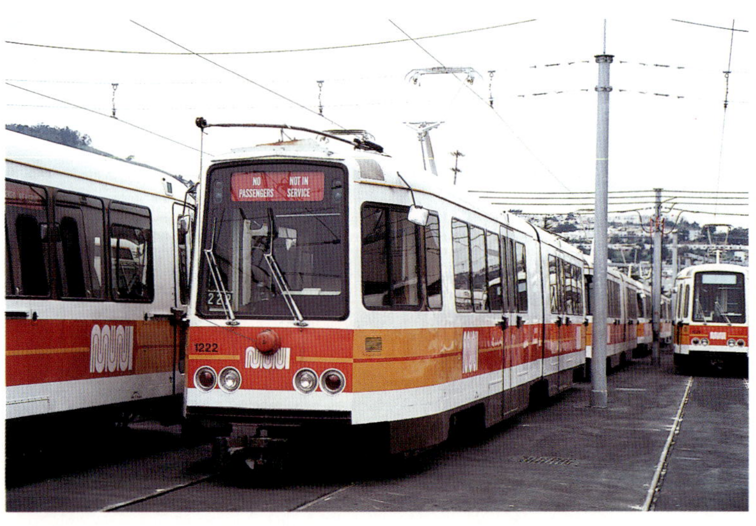

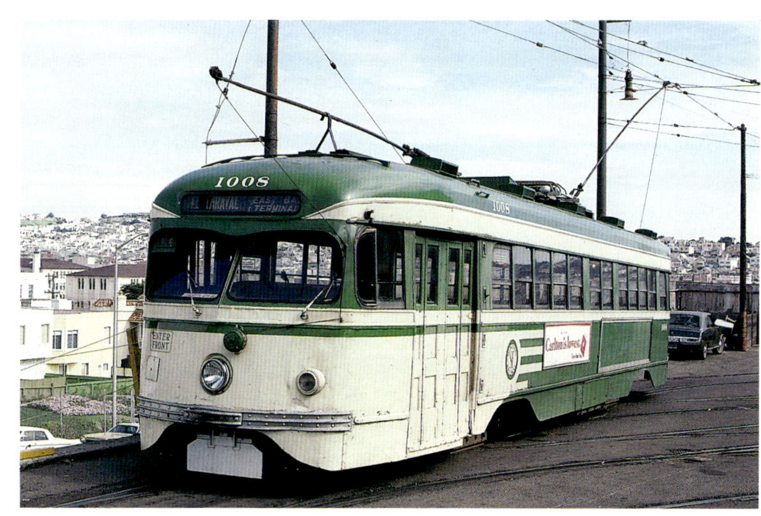

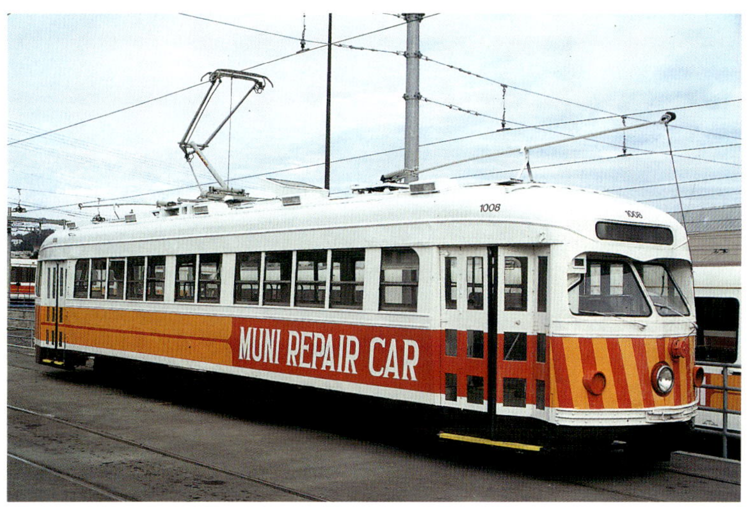

MUNI

(ABOVE LEFT & RIGHT) P.C.C. car No. 1008 was equipped with a pantograph and a viewing window midway along its roof in early 1978, so that engineers could evaluate overhead rebuilding work; in addition, a clearance template for the coupler height of the new L.R.V. fleet was placed under the front anticlimber for the purpose of testing coupler clearance on newly-rebuilt trackage. In late 1980, the car was converted into the Metro Division wrecker car-- seen here newly outshopped on November 21, 1980.

(BELOW LEFT & RIGHT) The Municipal Railway's line car No. 0304, shown in its old green paint scheme on West Portal Avenue in April 1979, was given a complete overhaul and a new paint job during 1983, as shown in the right photograph, in an effort to extend its service life.

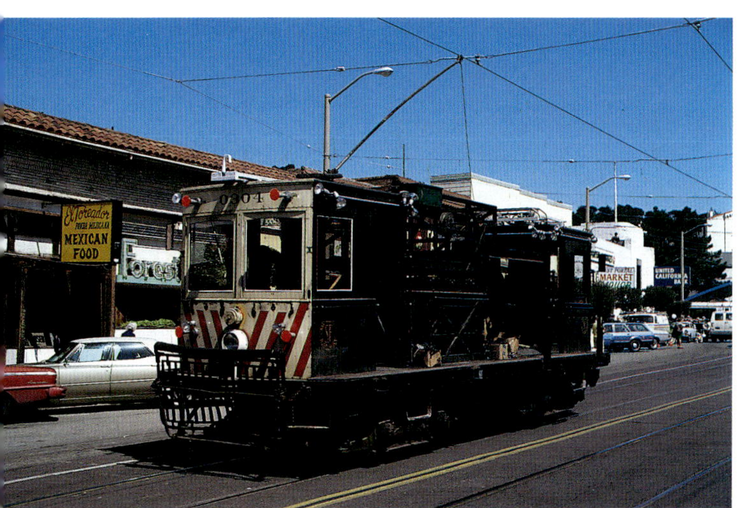

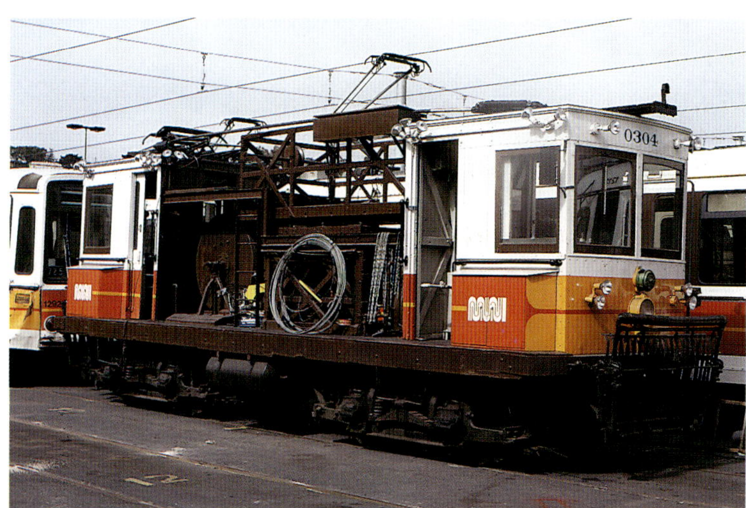

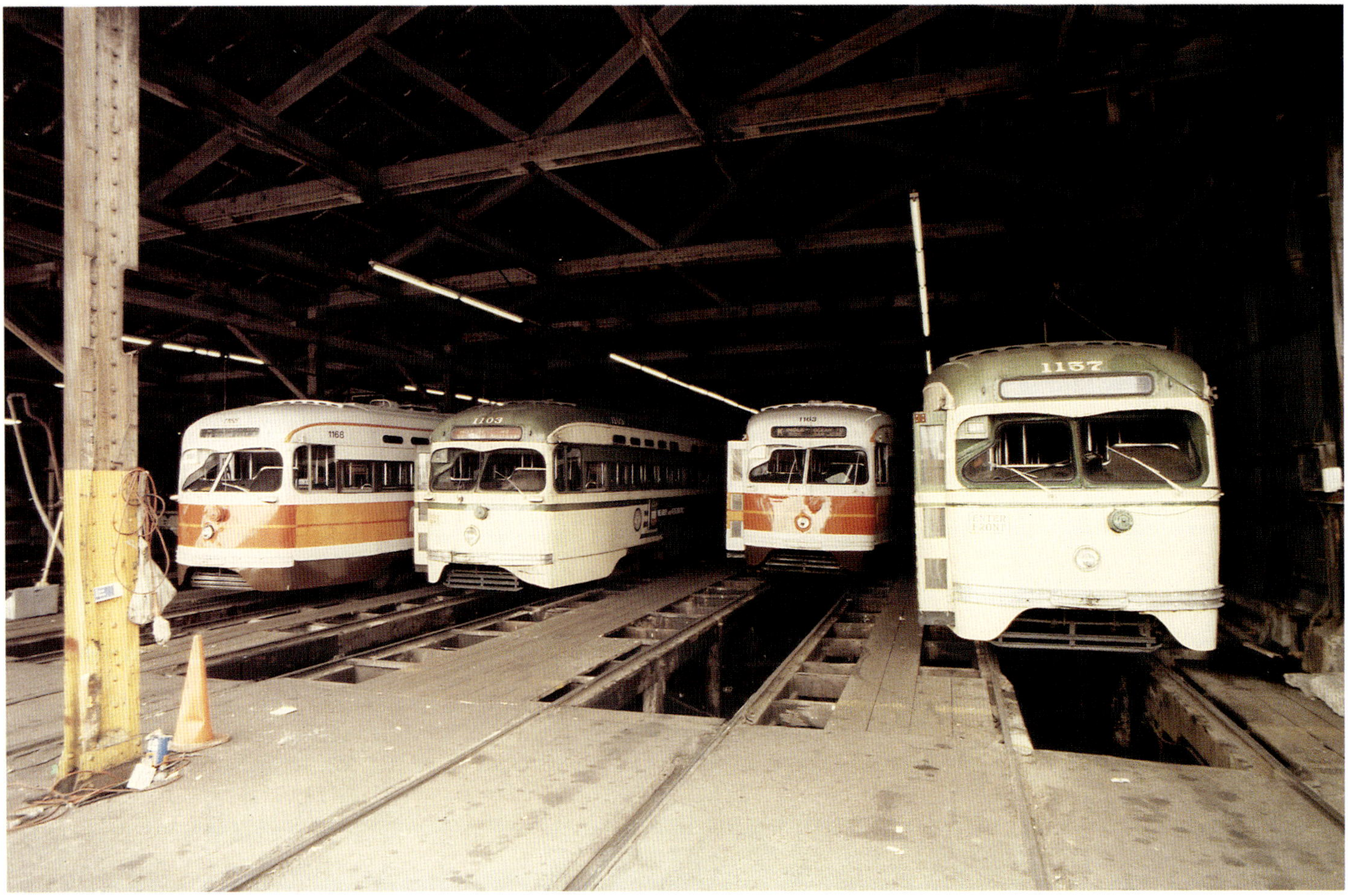

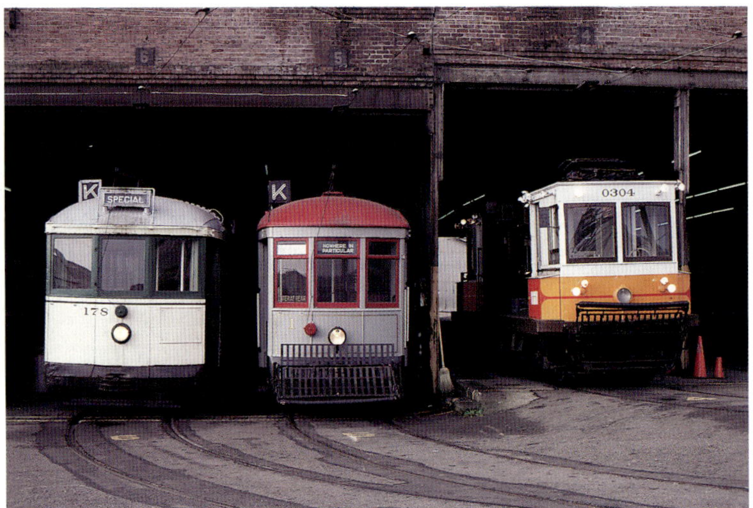

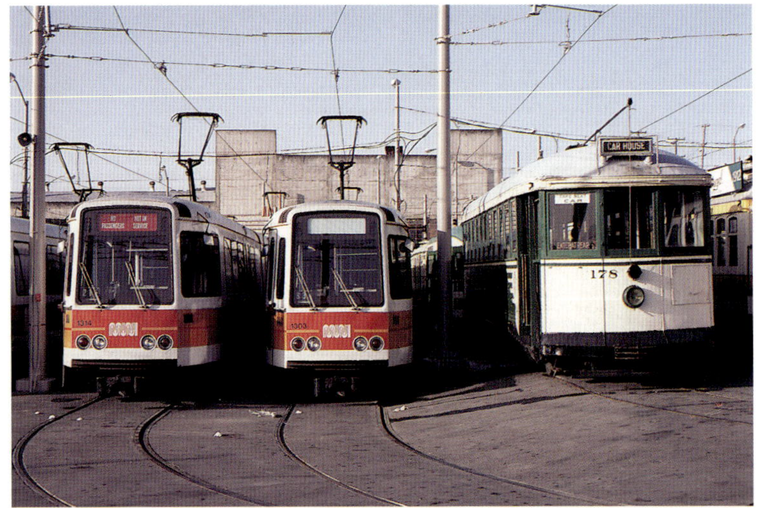

(ABOVE) Within the bays of the old Geneva Carbarn, shown here on November 30, 1978, light repairs and routine inspections kept Muni's P.C.C. fleet in serviceable condition until operations were transfered to the new Metro Center Shop in June 1979.
(MIDDLE LEFT) Posed together at the vintage carbarn on March 13, 1982, were venerable cars No. 178, No. 1, and No. 0304.
(LOWER LEFT) A scant three years later, on March 13, 1985, a similar-type view records the fact that much has changed at the site of the Geneva Carbarn. After demolition of the old structure, and the filling-in of the pits, a new storage yard was constructed upon the location of the old carbarn, but now the rail cars are stored outdoors.

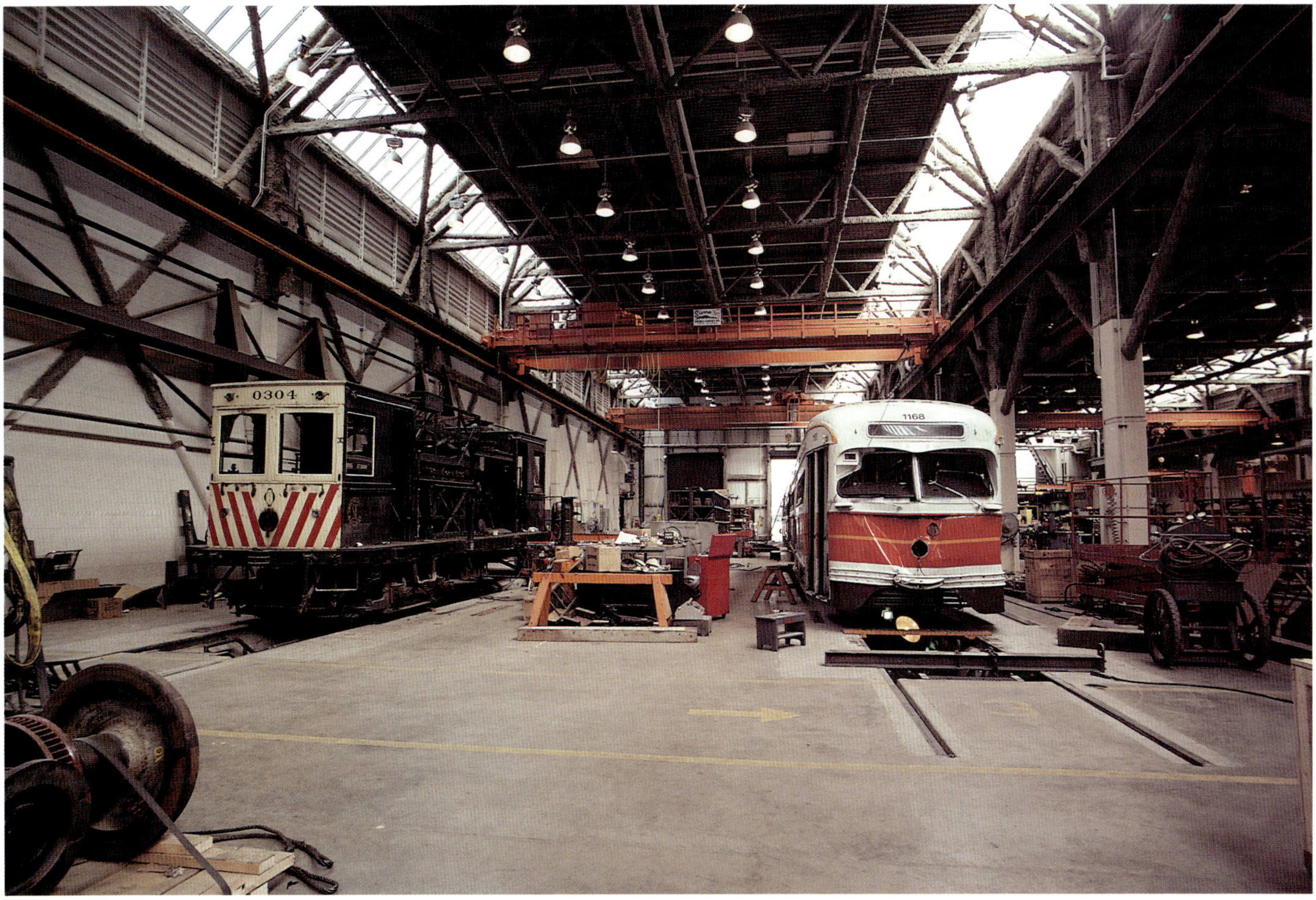

(ABOVE) The main workshop of the new Metro Center Shop, shown in February 1979, handles al1 heavy repair work for the Muni rail fleet.
(RIGHT) L.R.V. No. 1230, pictured here on October 18, 1987, demonstrates how the use of hydraulic lifting devices allow workers to change-out a car's trucks in a minimum amount of time.
(BELOW) Metro Center's running repair bay, seen on November 19, 1979, is where most normal light repairs and inspections are presently performed on the Municipal Railway L.R.V.s.

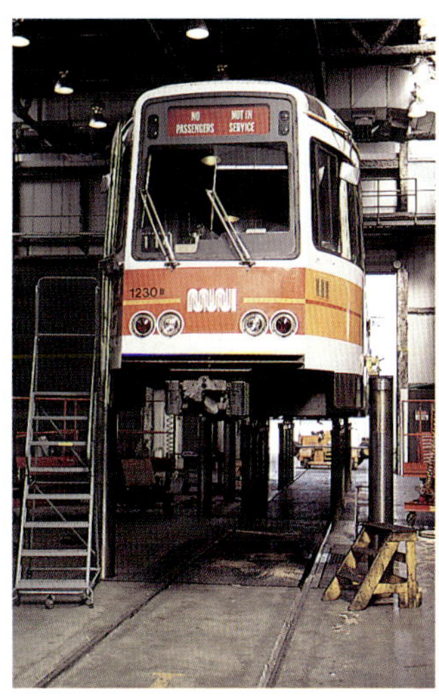

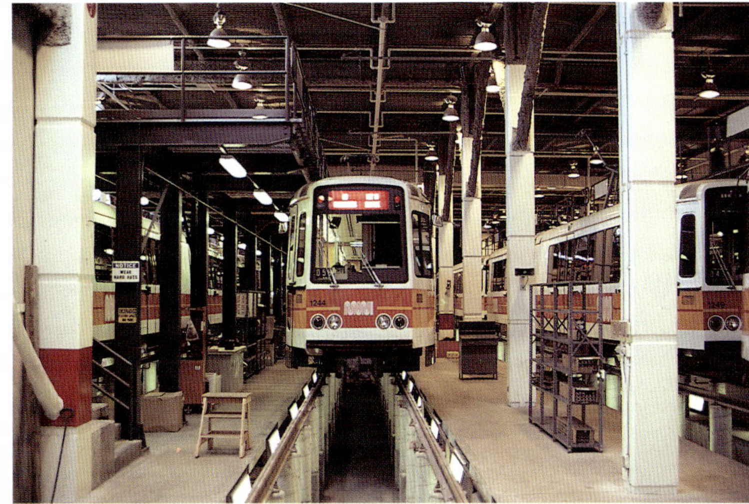

2

CABLE CAR DIVISION

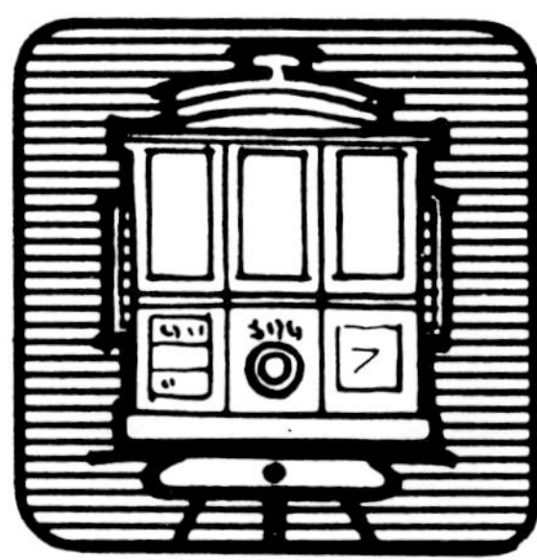

Perhaps no other single operation of the San Francisco Municipal Railway has undergone as complete an overhaul as did the organization's cable railway division during the mid-1980's. Due to a badly deteriorated cable trackway system, and for the need to upgrade 100-year old utility pipes along the cable car routes, it was decided to completely remove and rebuild every foot of cable railway track and track-support structures on the cable car system; in addition, it was felt that the wooden interior of the brick-clad cable car carbarn and powerhouse provided a potential fire threat to the operation of the historic service, and, therefore, during reconstruction of the trackage the powerhouse/carbarn building situated at Washington and Mason Streets would be gutted, with a new fireproof, reinforced concrete and steel building constructed behind the two street-side walls of the previous building.

With the complete shutdown of the city's cable car division on September 23, 1982, demolition, and then reconstruction, of the cable railway system was undertaken. The Muni's fleet of historic cable cars were stored in a massive warehouse along the waterfront, where, during the period of closure, all the car's wheels were changed-out due to the installation of new-type rails, with a different flange profile, upon the cable railway system. Along the three cable car lines the old cast iron track support devices (called "yokes" by cable railway personnel) were removed, as well as all of the old brick-lined cableways; once cleared of the old materials, new utility lines and pipes were installed, and then a new cable track support structure constructed entirely of reinforced concrete was put down to bring the streets up to the axle-loading requirements of today's automobiles, trucks, and buses. At the powerhouse, work was undertaken simultaneously to demolish, and then construct on the same site, the modernized powerhouse/shop facility designed as a replacement for the old structure. Among the improvements to the operation of the cable car system was the installation of separate electric motors to power each of the four 1¼"-diameter cables that provide propulsion for the cable cars on the three cable railway lines.

Upon completion of the rebuilding program, cable cars returned to the streets of San Francisco in June 1984. As popular as ever, the cable cars and the structures that they operate upon, are now guaranteed safe and reliable operation for the next 100 years.

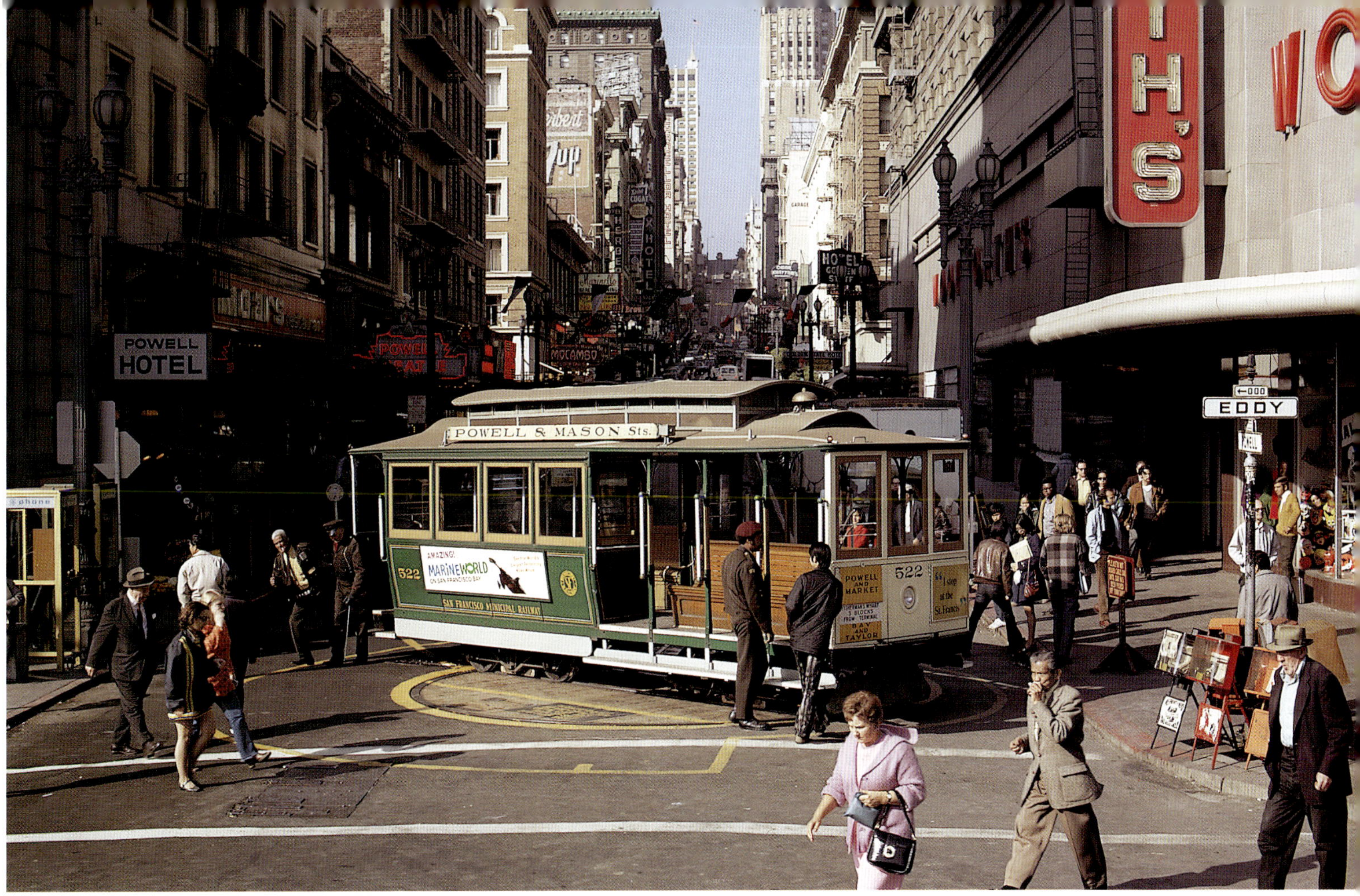

(ABOVE) Looking north along Powell Street, from Market Street, in October 1970, we note car No. 522 being turned in the time-honored tradition of San Francisco's cable railways-- atop the turntable at the end of the line. In the era of this photograph, the cable railway was still more of a regular part of the city's local transportation system, than the amusement park-like attraction that it has become.
(BELOW) Inbound California Street grip car No. 57 is just leaving the stop at Polk Street, as it carries off a load of happy passengers on September 19, 1982.

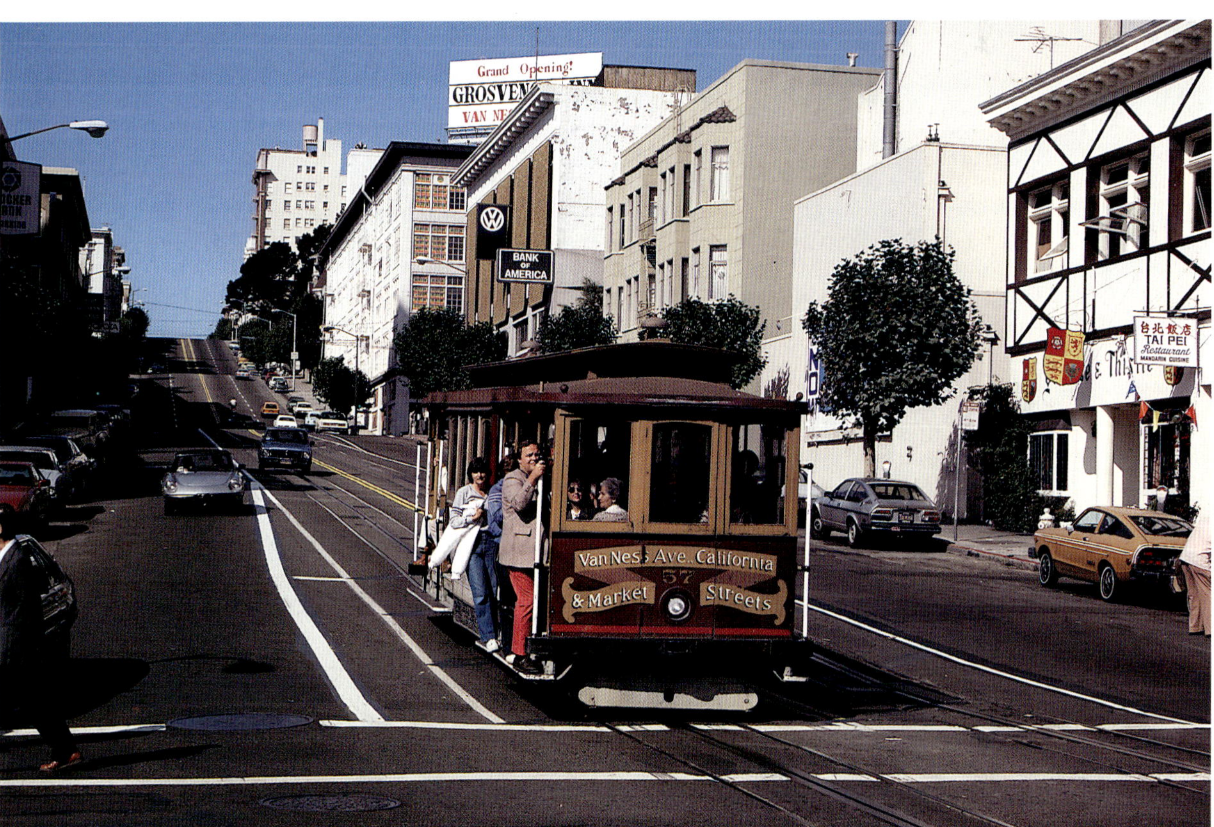

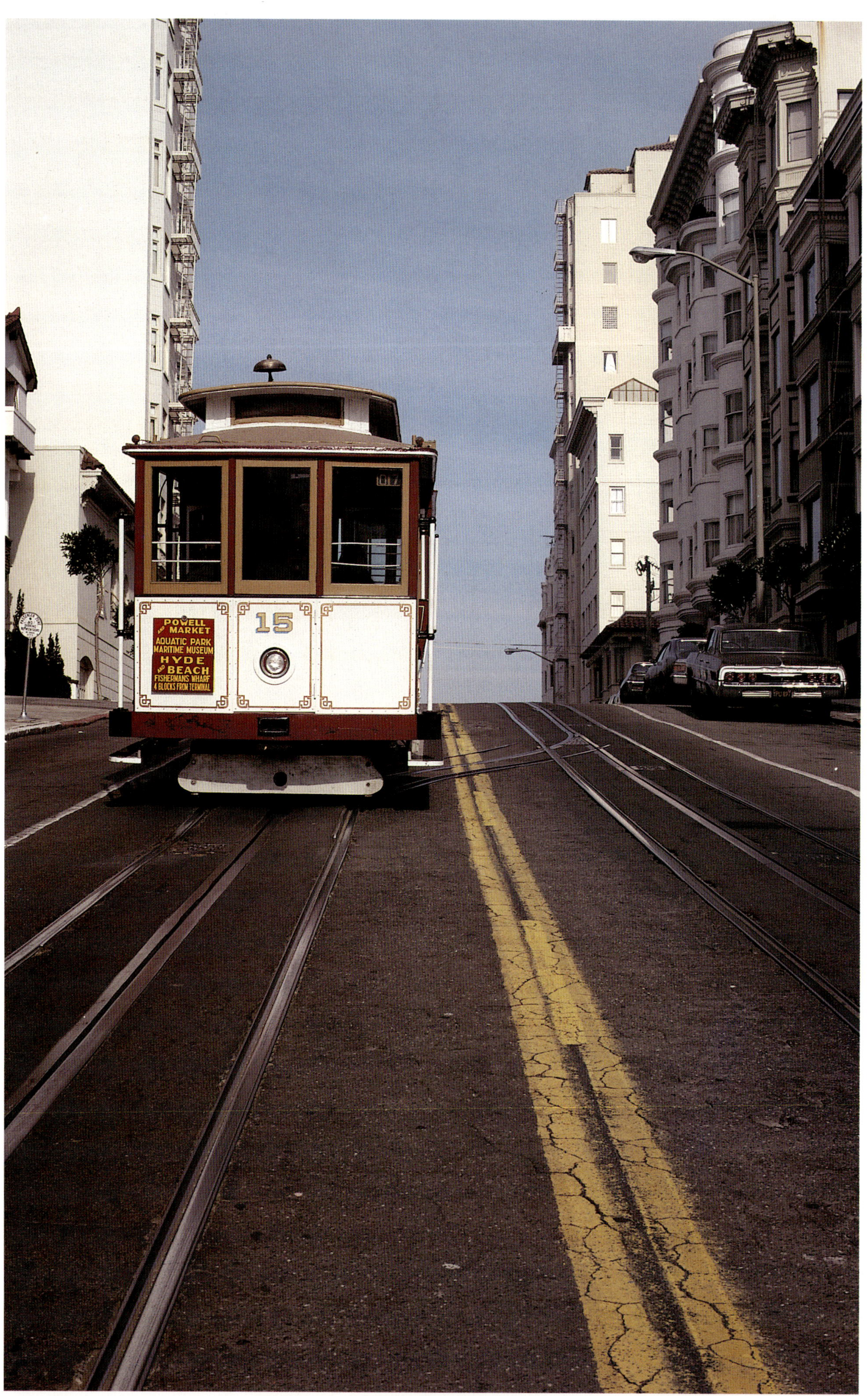
POWELL
AND MARKET
AQUATIC PARK
MARITIME MUSEUM
HYDE
AND BEACH
FISHERMANS WHARF
4 BLOCKS FROM TERMINAL
15

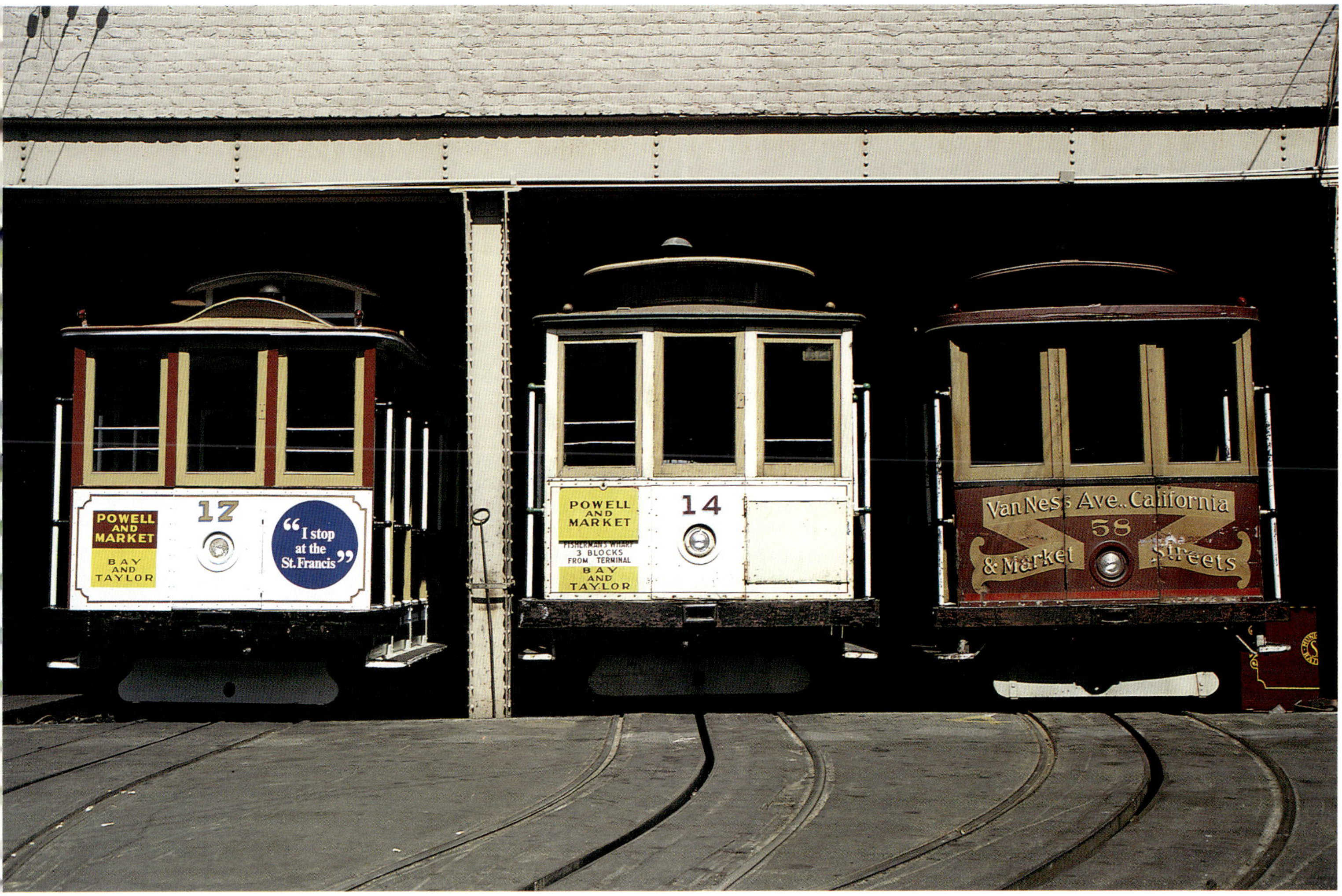

(OPPOSITE PAGE) Looking north along Hyde Street we observe southbound car No. 15 as it passes over the old California Street Cable Railway crossover, long unused, just north of Union Street, in February 1978. This section of the city, known as Russian Hill, is one of the town's premier residential neighborhoods.

(ABOVE) Facing east from the old turntable in the now-vanished open storage yard at the Washington-Mason cable car carbarn, we observe cars Nos. 17, 14, and 58-- each painted in a different paint scheme. Car No. 17 is attired in the original Powell Street Railway livery, while car No. 14 carries the traditional San Francisco Municipal Railway green and cream colors; car No. 58, on the right, sports the customary red livery of the California Street cable line on this bright July 24, 1979, afternoon.

(RIGHT) Rarely seen, but even more rarely used, was the transfer table on the ground floor of the old carbarn/powerhouse building; the elevator that connected the lower and upper floors was another seldom-used feature of the old building. Due to the rebuilding of the storage yard turntable, in the spring of 1970, both of those facilities were reactivated for a few days during the construction period.

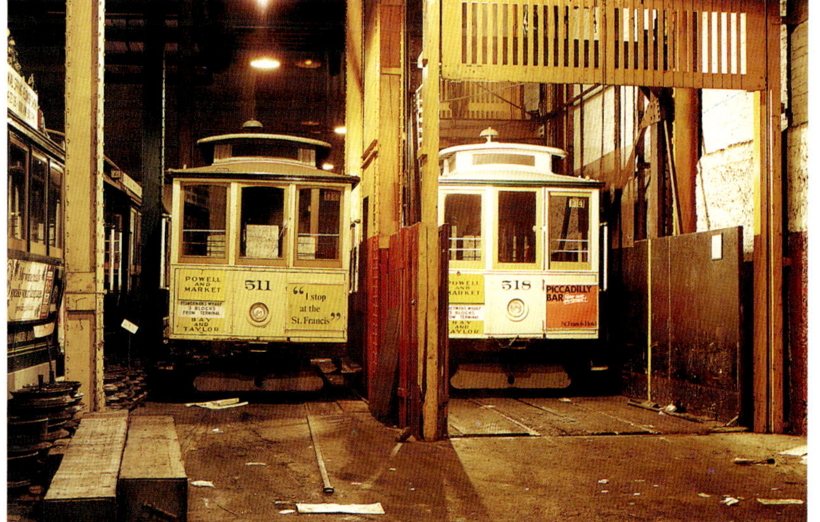

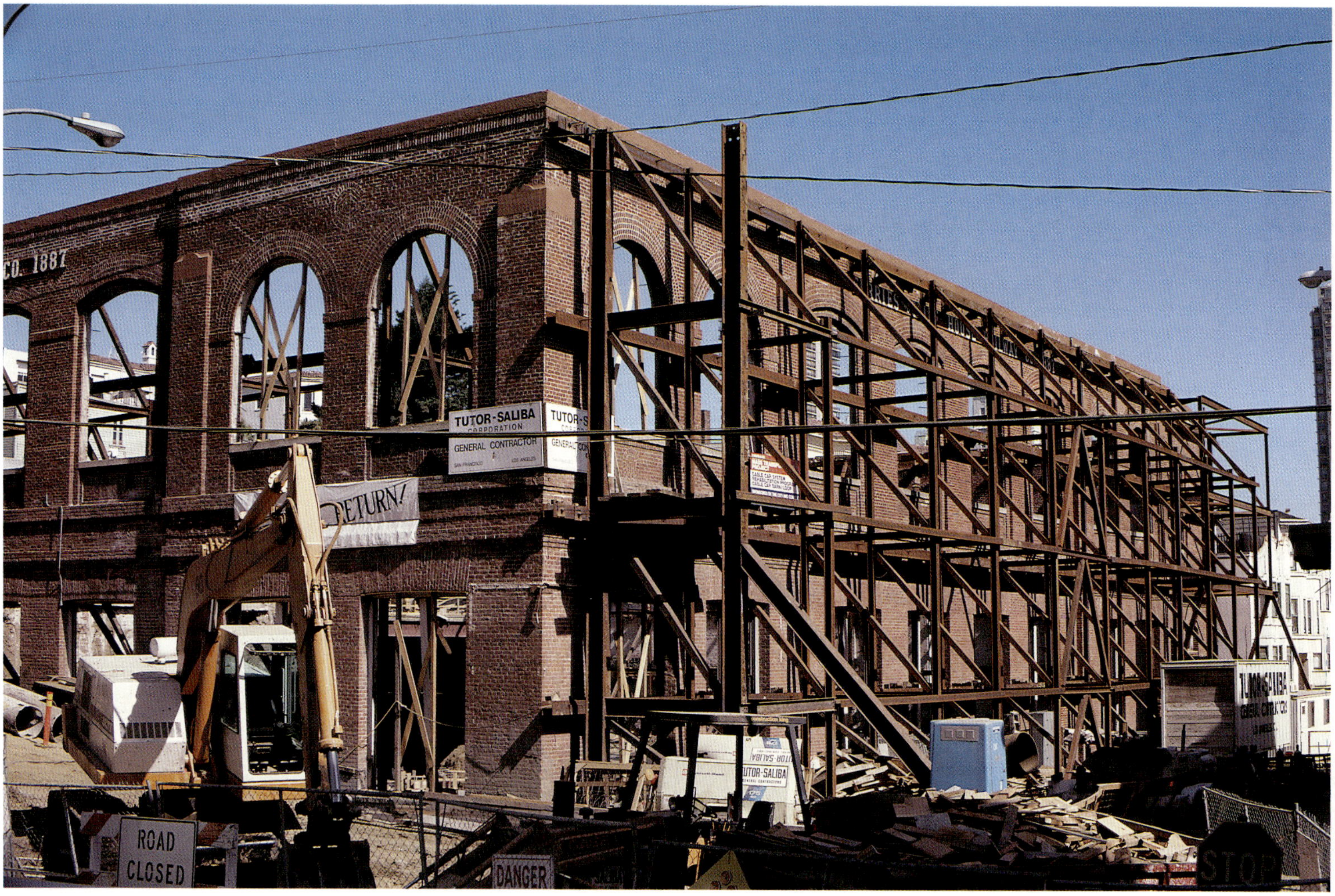

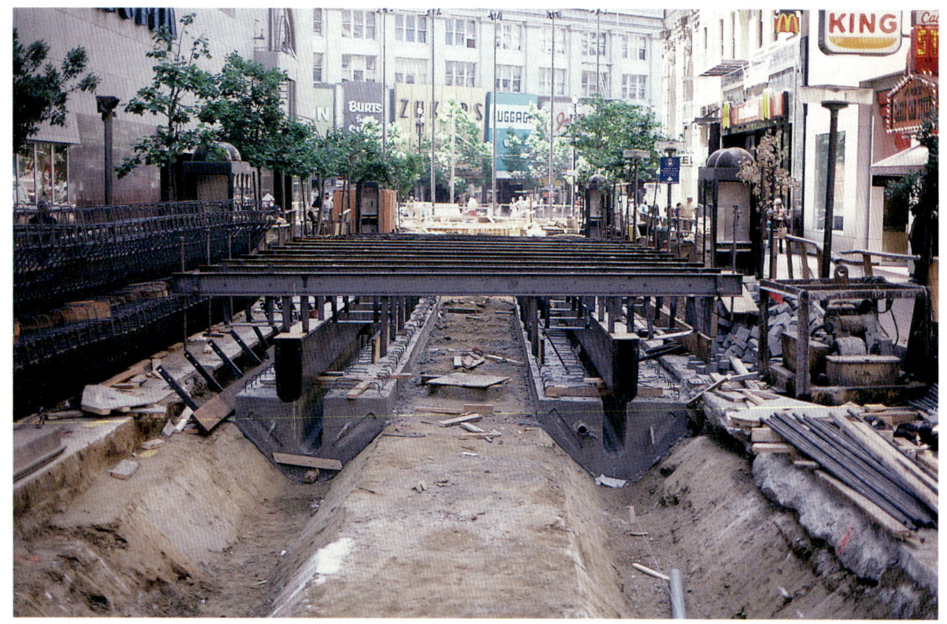

(ABOVE) Here we see just how it was possible to preserve the vintage exterior walls of the Washington-Mason powerhouse/carbarn during the reconstruction of the cable railway system. We face north along Mason Street, from Washington Street, on June 19, 1983.

(LEFT) When looking south along Powell Street from Ellis Street, on June 12, 1983, one was able to observe the construction methods employed to create the new reinforced-concrete cable trackway structure which supplanted the old brick and cast iron trackways on the rebuilt system.

(OPPOSITE PAGE) Cable car No. 23 is photographed as it makes a test run over newly-installed trackage on Jackson Street, during an unusually clear day in May 1984. The handsome car rests at Mason Street while the gripman takes the rope prior to ascending the grade toward Hyde Street, and while the pointed top of the Transamerica Pyramid glistens in the afternoon sun.

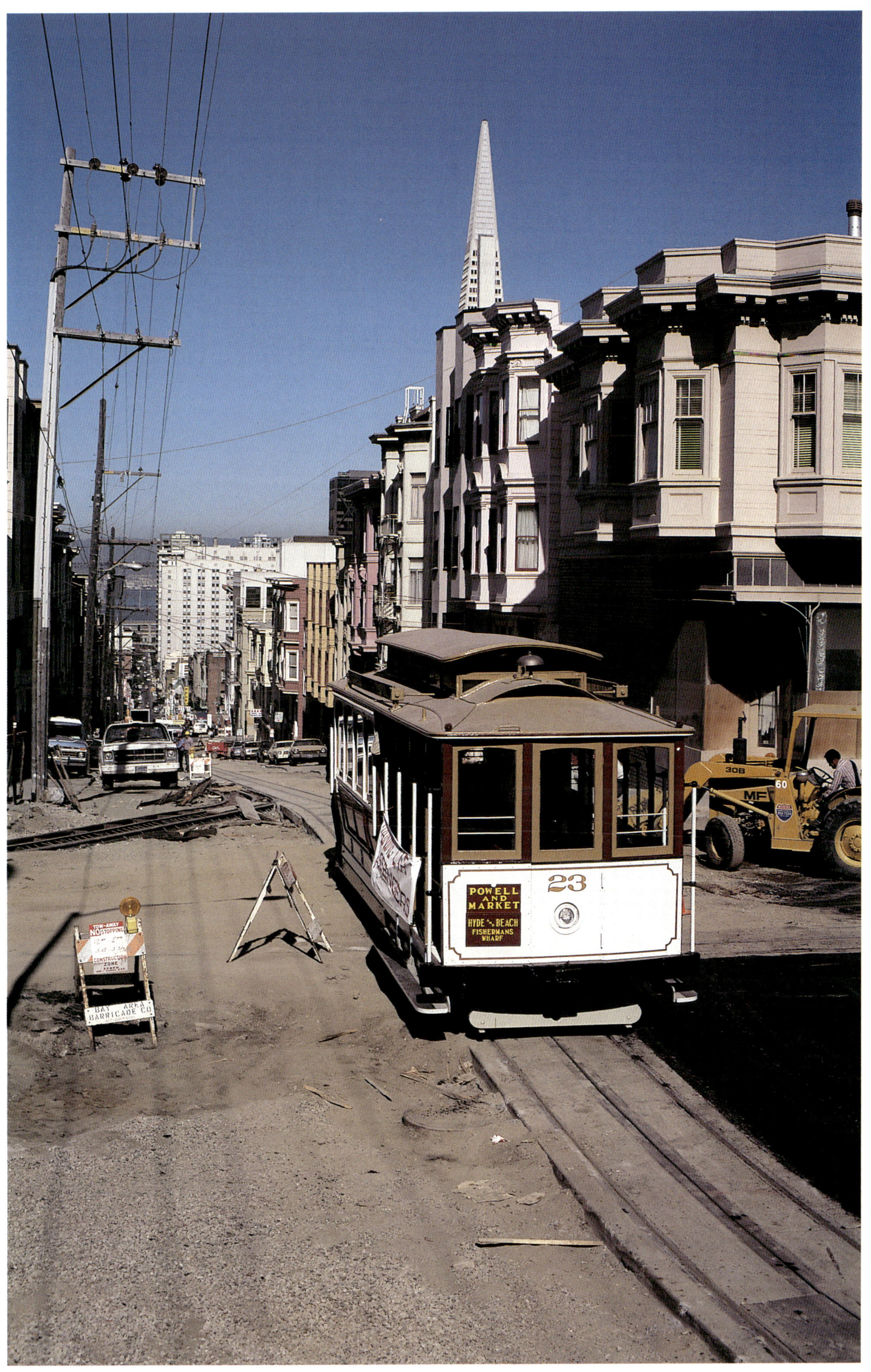
TOW-AWAY
NO STOPPING
CONSTRUCTION ZONE
BAY AREA
BARRICADE CO
23
POWELL AND MARKET
HYDE AND BEACH
FISHERMANS WHARF
30B
MF
60

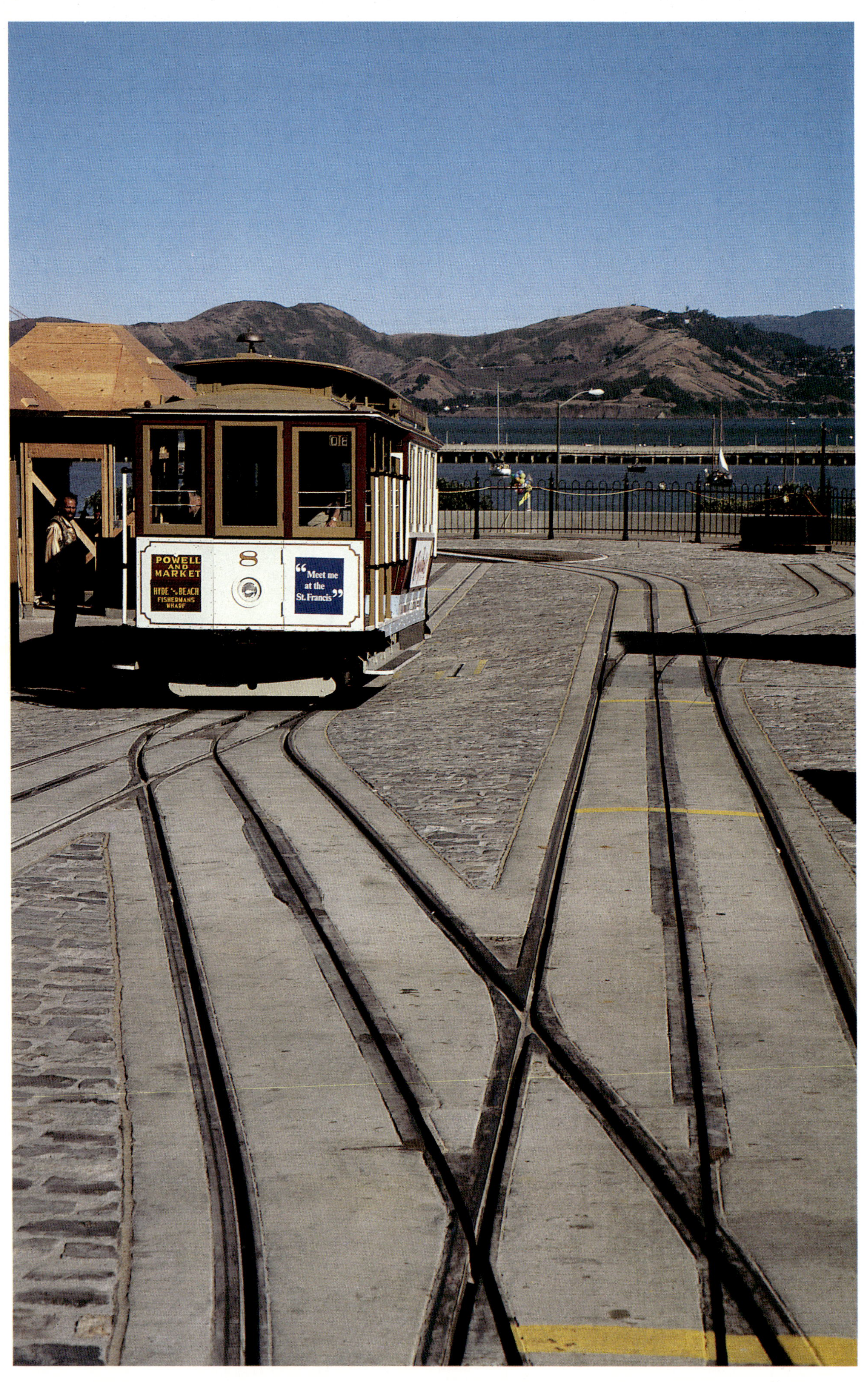
POWELL AND MARKET
HYDE BEACH
FISHERMANS WHARF
8
"Meet me at the St. Francis"

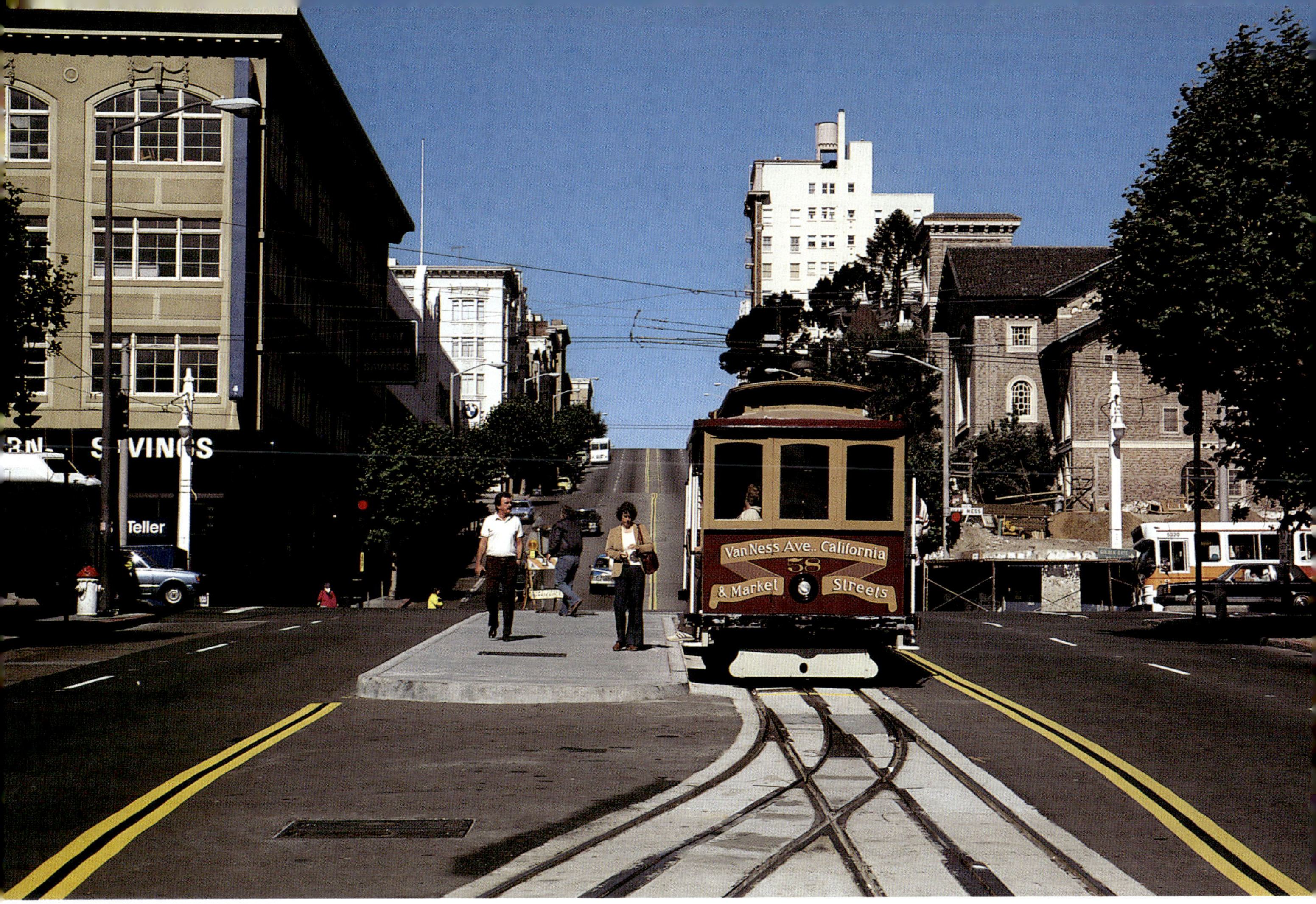

(ABOVE) Car No. 58, resplendent in a shiny new paint job, awaits departure time at the rebuilt cable car system's new passenger loading platform located on the east side of Van Ness Avenue at California Street. The date is June 1984, and we are witnessing the first revenue operation on a Sunday of the re-opened cable railway line.
(OPPOSITE PAGE) The changes at the northern terminal of the Hyde Street cable line are more dramatic than a mere rebuilding of the former facilities. As our photograph demonstrates, a crossover for the possible use of double-ended California Street grip cars on this line, and a stub-end storage track for the side-lining of disabled equipment, have been added to the track arrangement at this locale. With the hills of Marin County as a background, here is car No. 8 about to depart on its way downtown on June 9, 1985.

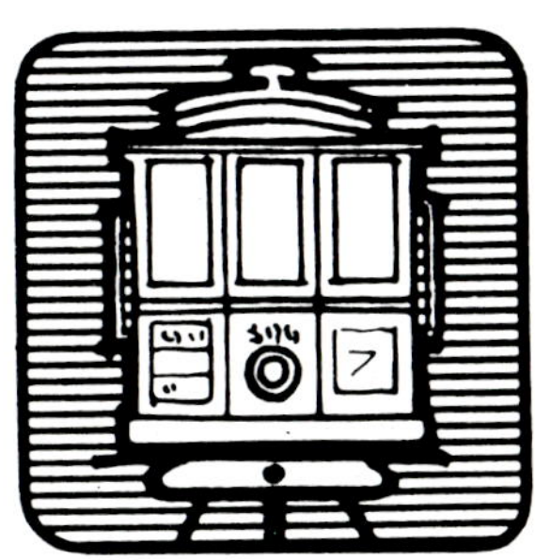

3

TROLLEY COACHES

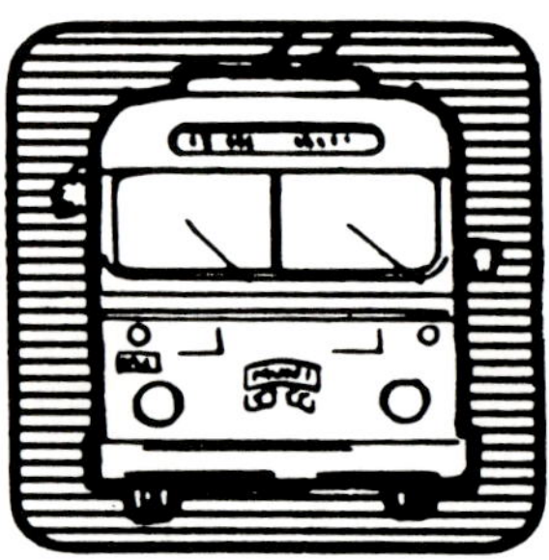

The large fleet of quiet, ordorless electric trolley coaches operated today by San Francisco's Municipal Railway owes its existence to the far-sightedness of early-day City Engineer Marsden Manson, who championed the development of San Francisco's Hetch-Hetchy water and hydroelectric project in the early years of this century. Because of the relatively inexpensive cost of providing electric power to its inhabitants, through city-owned power generating stations situated in the far-off valleys of the Sierra Nevada mountain range, use of electric transit buses in San Francisco has grown constantly since their introduction on the Market Street Railway's line No. 33 on October 6, 1935.

Today, there are 345 Canadian-built electric trolley coaches stabled on the Municipal Railway roster; these are all single-body, two-axle vehicles, each propelled by a single traction motor. However, Muni has recently awarded a contract to purchase its first group of high-capacity, articulated trolley buses, these to be equipped with solid-state control apparatus and two alternating current traction motors.

Plans are presently being drawn up to convert the diesel bus-operated line No. 31 to a trolley coach service when a number of present electric buses are made surplus upon the arrival of the new articulated coaches; long-term planning for the conversion to electric power of other diesel bus lines is also taking place at this time, with the implementation of these plans only being contingent upon the availability of adequate funding. With other California cities, including Los Angeles and Sacramento, eyeing the reintroduction of trolley coaches as a part of their transit operations, San Francisco can be proud of the fact that it has been an industry leader in the operation and maintenance of those environment-enhancing vehicles upon its extensive transit network.

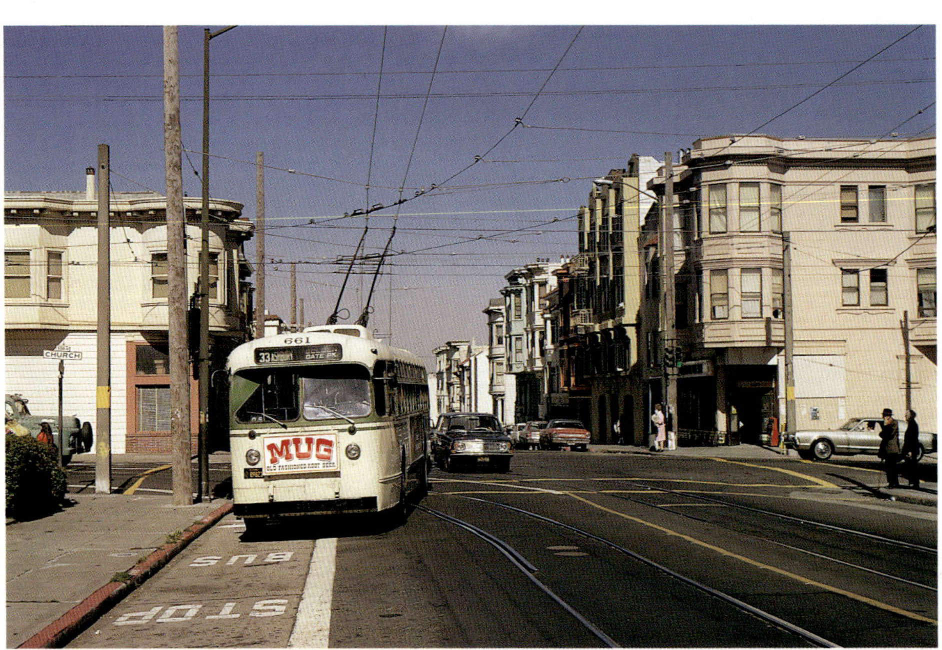

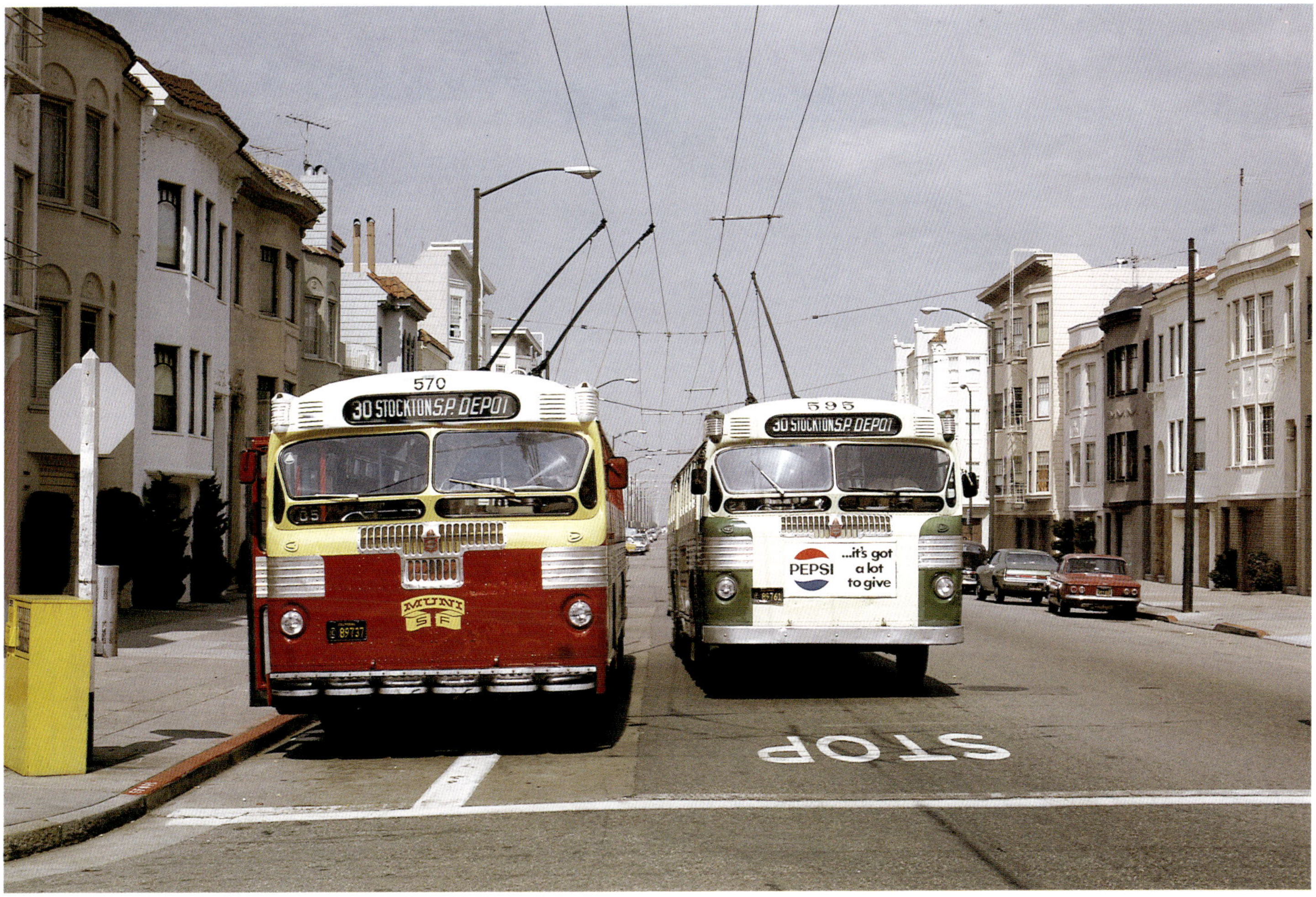

(ABOVE) Municipal Railway trolley coach No. 570 was given a complete electrical overhaul and a modified version of the paint scheme applied to Muni's new diesel fleet during the late 1960's, in a one-of-a-kind upgrading in late 1969. Here that coach lays over on Divisadero Street, at Chestnut Street, while in service on line No. 30 in March 1970; coach No. 595, another Fageol-Twin trolley coach, passes enroute to the S.P. Station.

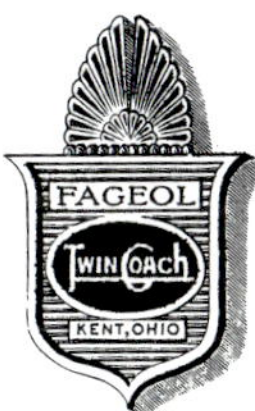

(RIGHT) A number of Muni trolley buses were sold to Mexico City for further use after the arrival of new coaches in San Francisco. At Servicio De Transportes Electricos Del Distrito Federal's Azcapotzalco shop/carbarn, we see a former Municipal Railway Marmon-Herrington coach posed next to a well-used Mexico City P.C.C. car in December 1978.

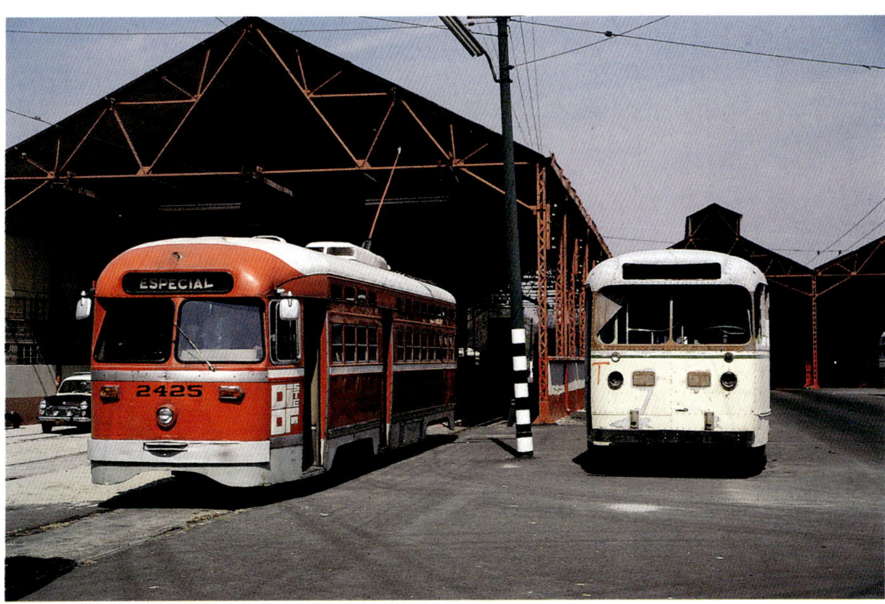

(OPPOSITE PAGE) Looking eastward along 17th Street, at Church Street, we witness the arrival of line No. 33's coach No. 661 at the passenger loading zone in January 1974. The temporary re-routing of line No. 33 off 18th Street was due to B.A.R.T.D. construction down Mission Street, and a number of changes to Muni trolley coach services to permit continued operation of electric buses during the B.A.R.T.D. building program.

Southbound L.R.V. No. 1213, in Trolley Festival service, passes trolley coach No. 5128 of line No. 21 on Market Street, just south of Montgomery Street, on July 3, 1983. In this photograph, trolley wires for both trolley coaches and streetcars are as they have been for many years; beginning in late 1985, all trolley overhead wires were completely replaced, with a new trolley coach lane installed over the streetcar tracks-- bringing back four lane traction action to the city's main thoroughfare. While one can no longer hear the "roar of the four," today it is possible to "navigate the eight!"

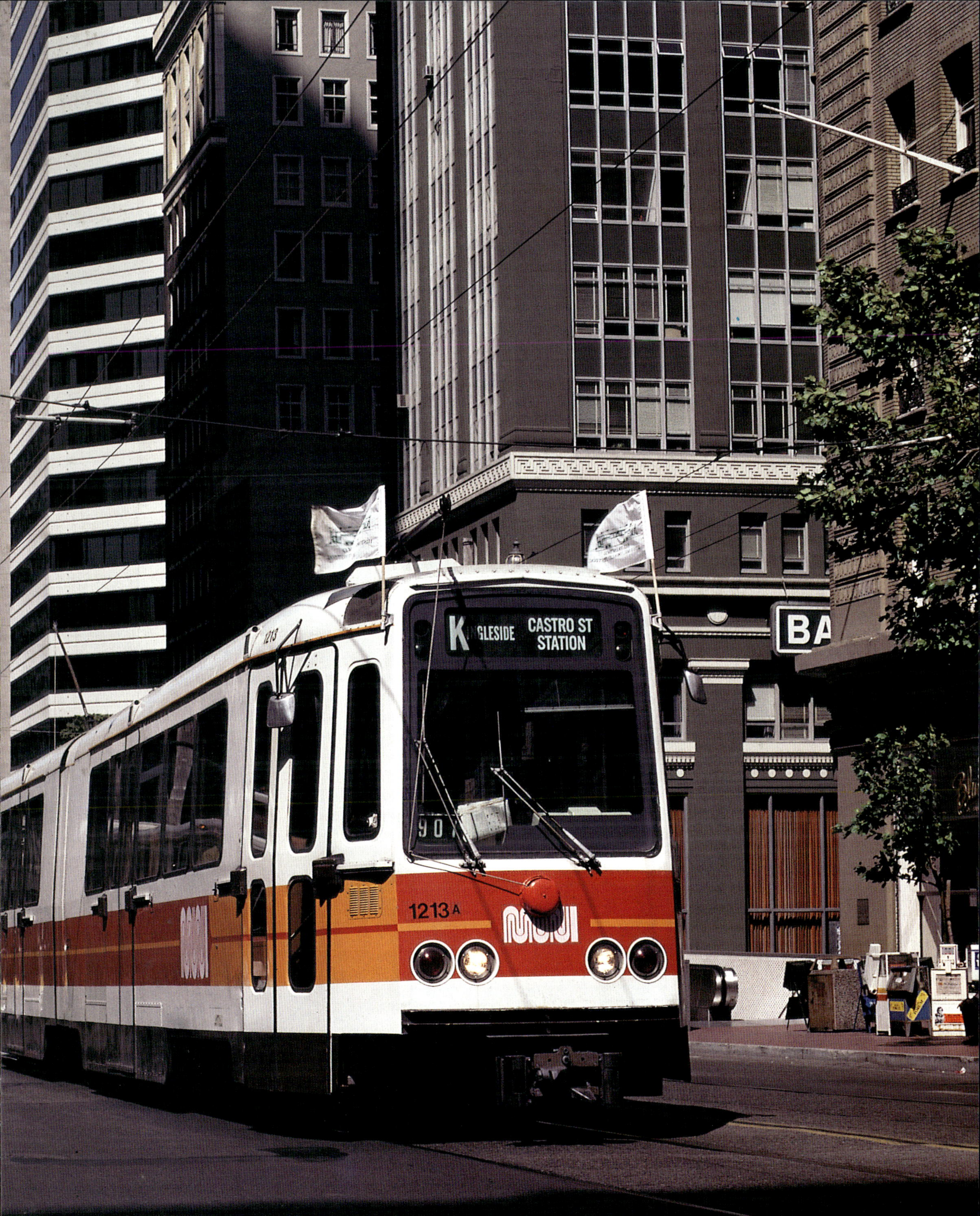

K
CASTRO ST
STATION
1213
1213 A
BA

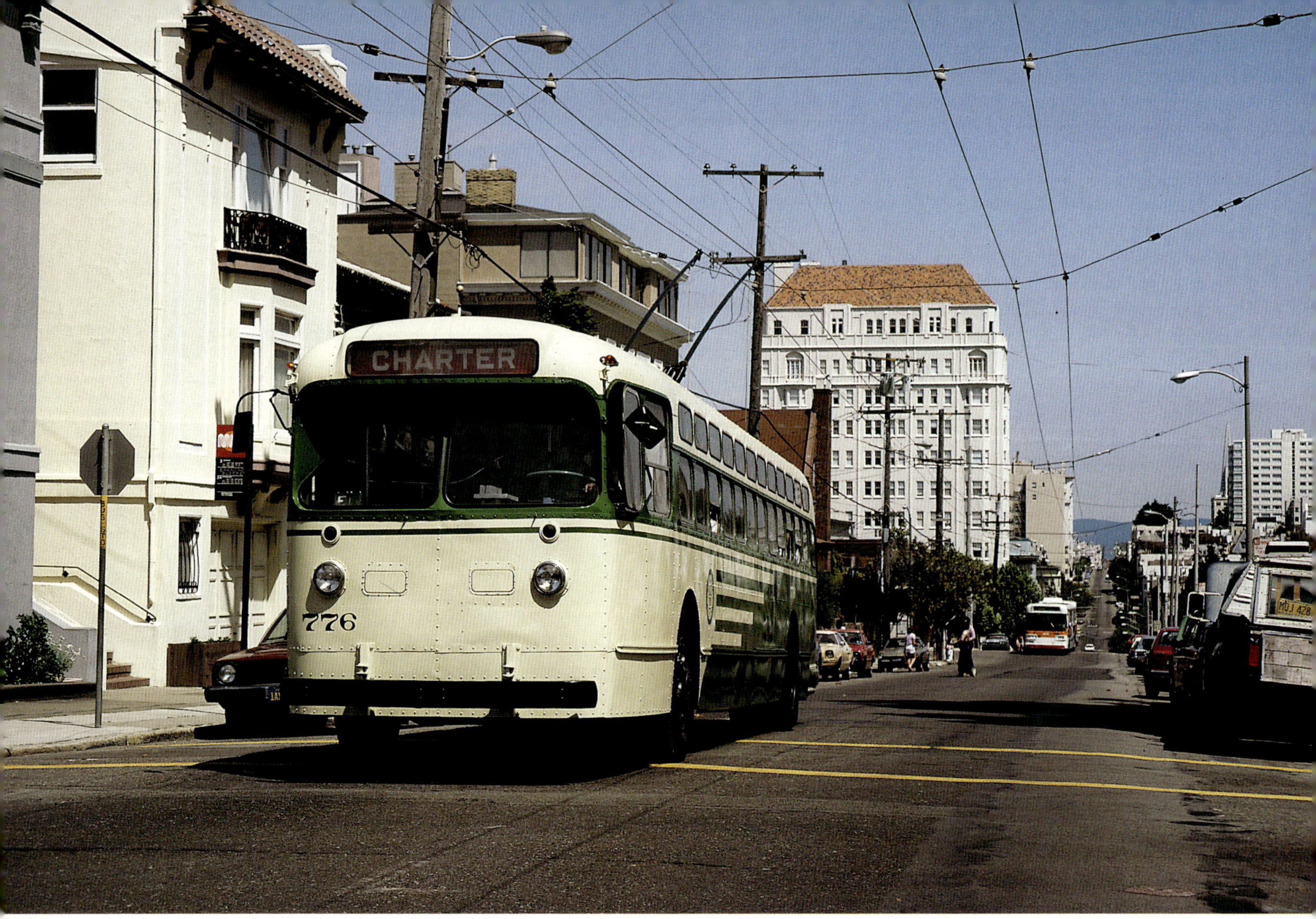

(ABOVE) A private excursion aboard historic trolley coach No. 776, on Augus 21, 1983, gave riders a preview of the newly-completed electrification of diesel bus-operated line No. 24. In this view we witness the classic vehicle heading westbound along Jackson Street, at Scott Street. A regular service electric coach, on line No. 3, is seen in the background on this beautiful day.

(RIGHT) Later that afternoon the excursion coach poses, again headed westbound, on 30th Street between Church and Chenery Streets.

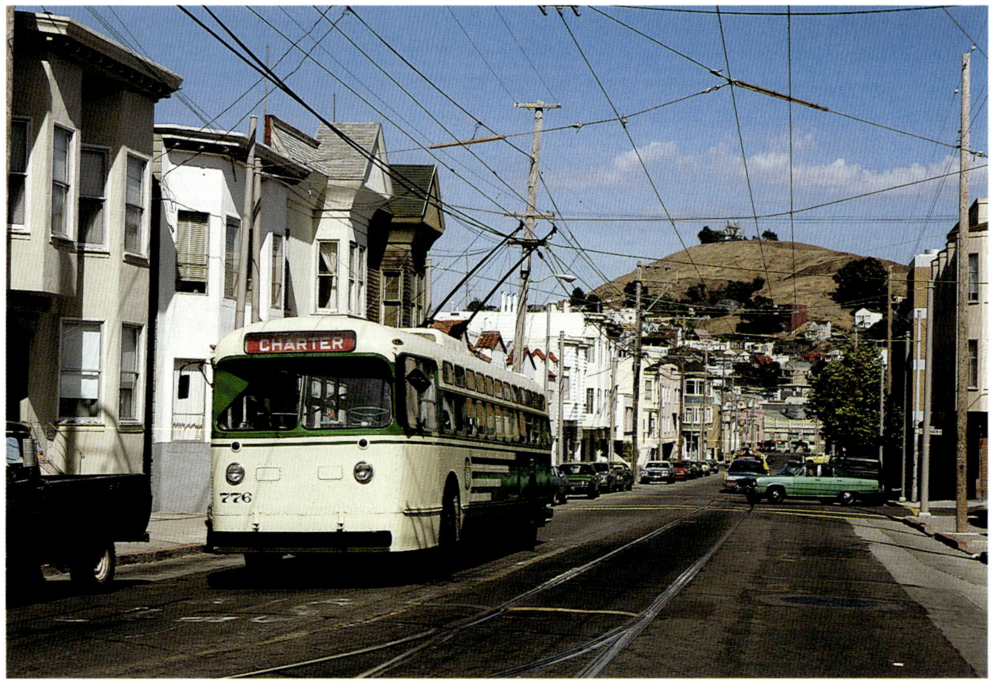

The first articulated trolley bus to be demonstrated over the electrified lines of the Municipal Railway, was this colorful Crown-Ikarus coach seen at Potrero Yard on June 30, 1982.

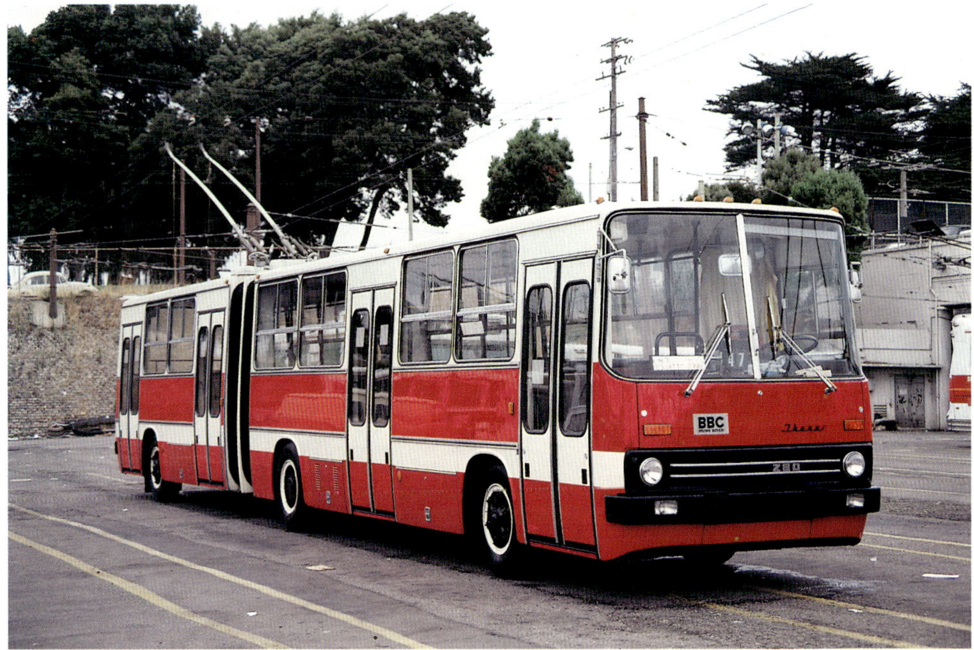

A second articulated bus tried upon the trolley coach network was this impressive vehicle, photographed at Potrero Division on January 27, 1986, and which was manufactured by Neoplan.

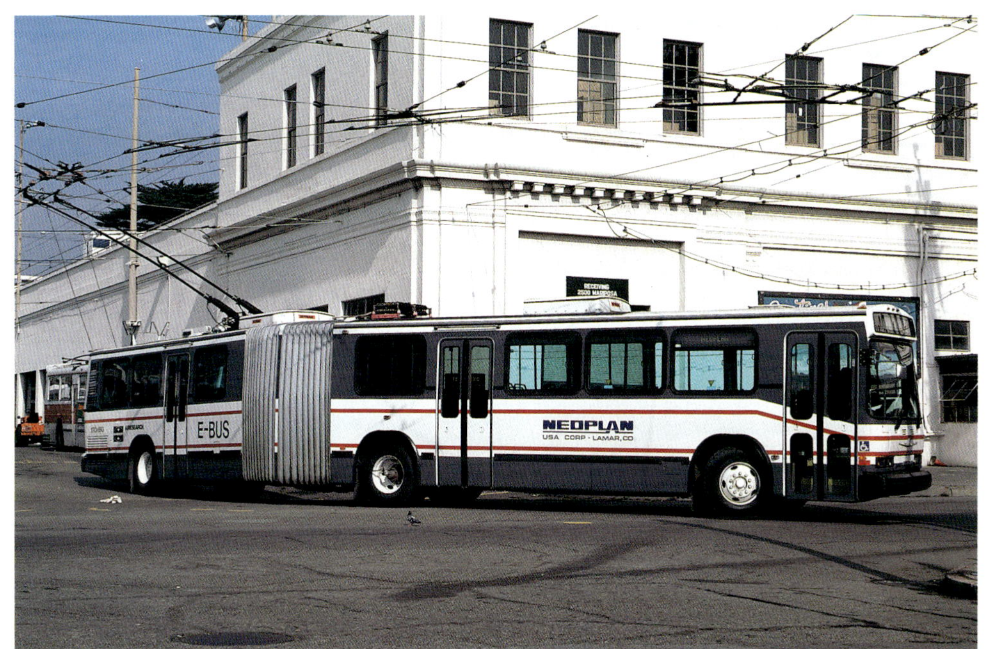

Muni trolley coach No. 5161 was temporarily outfitted with a manufacturer's solid-state control system, for demonstration and evaluation purposes, that featured a large roof-mounted bank of resistor grids. That coach is shown here at the Presidio Yard, on December 10, 1984.

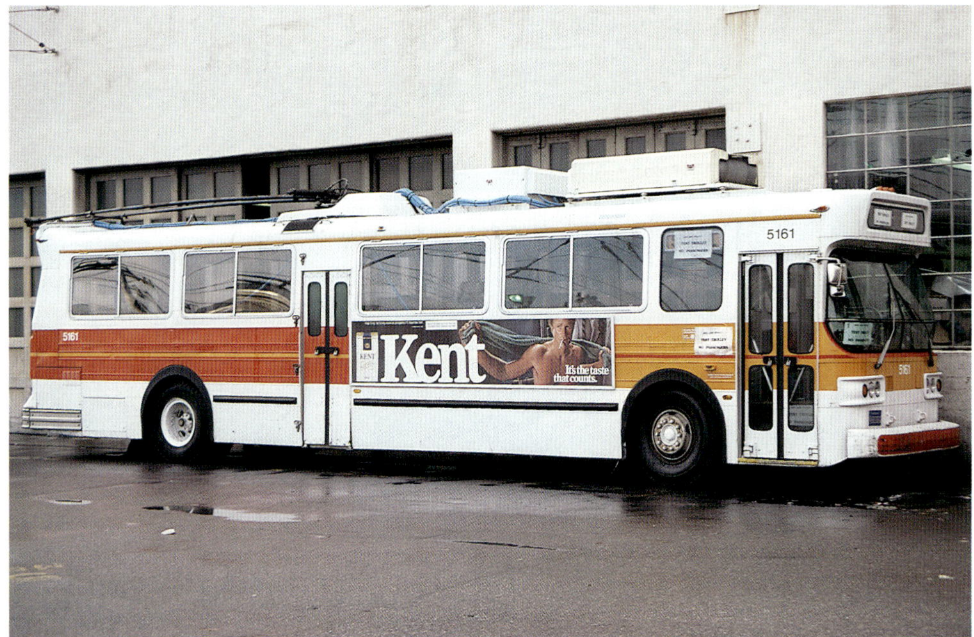

4

MOTOR COACHES

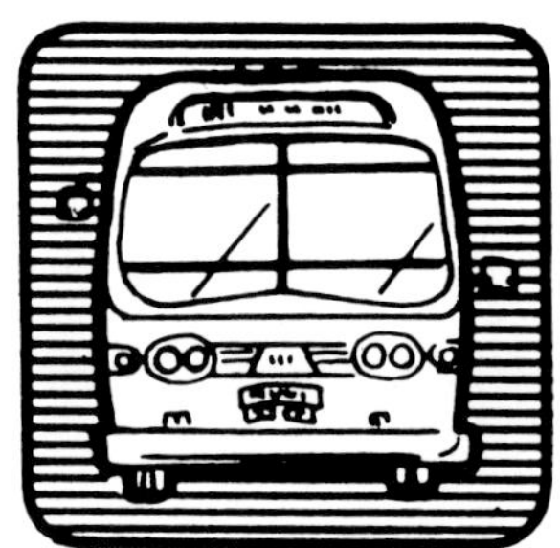

Though the diesel-powered transit bus was once hailed as the saviour of the public transit industry, it now appears that the continued use of those type of vehicles within the state of California is nearing an end. Because of concerns over environmential harm, and the revelation that the automotive industry decived the public on facts concerning just how harmful diesel engine exhaust emissions really are, the search is on for alternative energy sources less harmful to the health of the planet and its inhabitants.

The San Francisco Municipal Railway, with over 40 separate transit routes utilizing diesel-powered vehicles, has taken the lead in seeking to replace the noisy, odoriferous conveyances with electrically-powered coaches. However, until a suitable replacement is found to supplant the fuel utilized in its roster of diesel buses, the Municipal Railway will be forced to continue operating its present fleet of internal combustion coaches. The current roster of such vehicles includes buses manufactured by New Flyer Industries, General Motors, Orion, A.M. General, and the German concern, M.A.N.

Perhaps it is a bit optimistic to envision a day when San Francisco is finally free of its loud, smelly, diesel motor coaches, but that goal is not entirely out of the question. Transit planners forsee a fleet of rubber-tired, battery-powered transit vehicles, in conjunction with additional coaches powered by other, less harmful, fuels such as natural gas, propane, or methanol, as a solution to the diesel fuel problem. Thus, San Francisco could certainly be among the leaders of the emerging clean air movement, and among the first transit agencies to totally replace that menace to air quality, the diesel engine.

East meets West: Muni purchased the front section of a former New York City bus for utilization in the rebuilding of badly-wrecked coach No. 3057; after joining portions of the two bodies together, this is what that vehicle looked like prior to entering the paint shop. Photo taken at the Woods Division body shop on February 25, 1982.

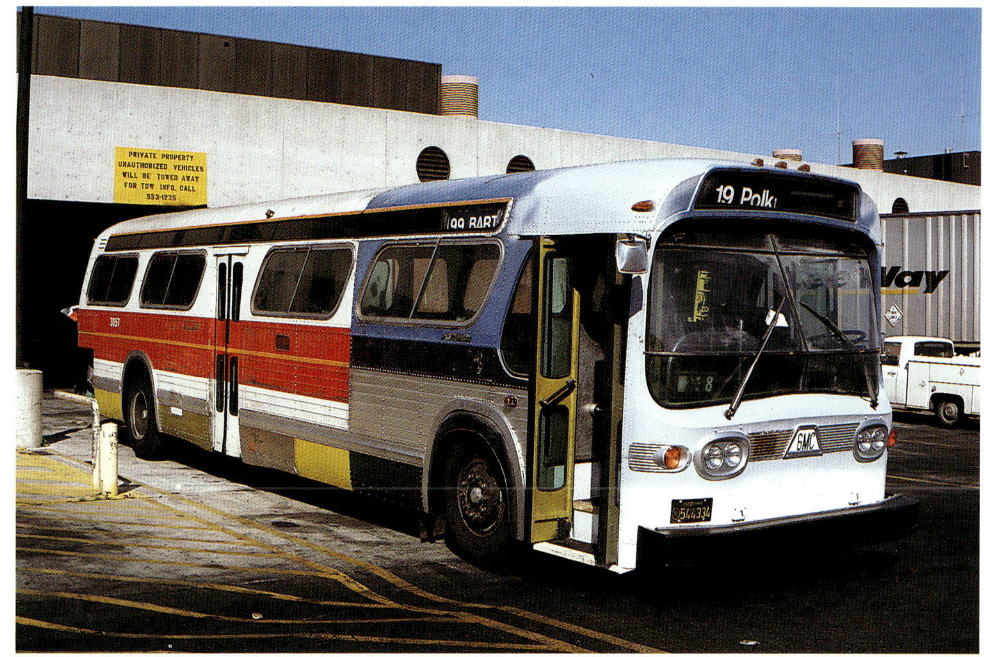

To help improve service reliability on line No. 80x, a rush hour line ferrying riders between the Caltrain rail commuter station and downtown San Francisco, the Municipal Railway operated a small fleet of Caltrain-leased A.C.Transit buses in the early 1980's. Here is one of those vehicles, No. 2765, posed at Woods Division on January 21, 1985.

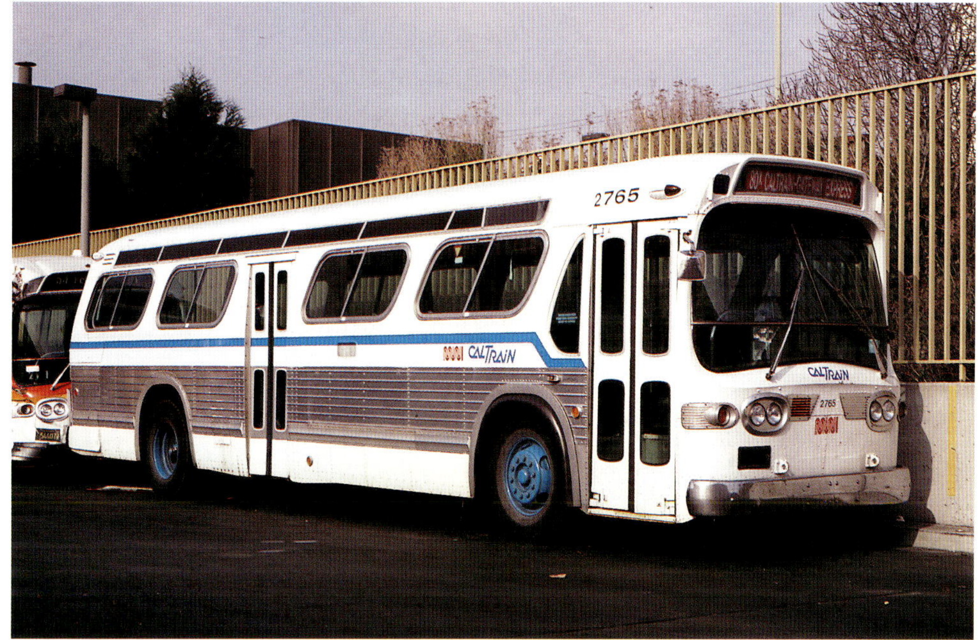

They just don't make patrol cars large enough for today's law enforcement needs, so former Muni coach No. 3640 has been transformed into the city's biggest police car! Actually, and in reality, that bus, photographed at Woods Yard on February 13, 1990, is used to transport city police to parades, civil demonstrations, and other such events.

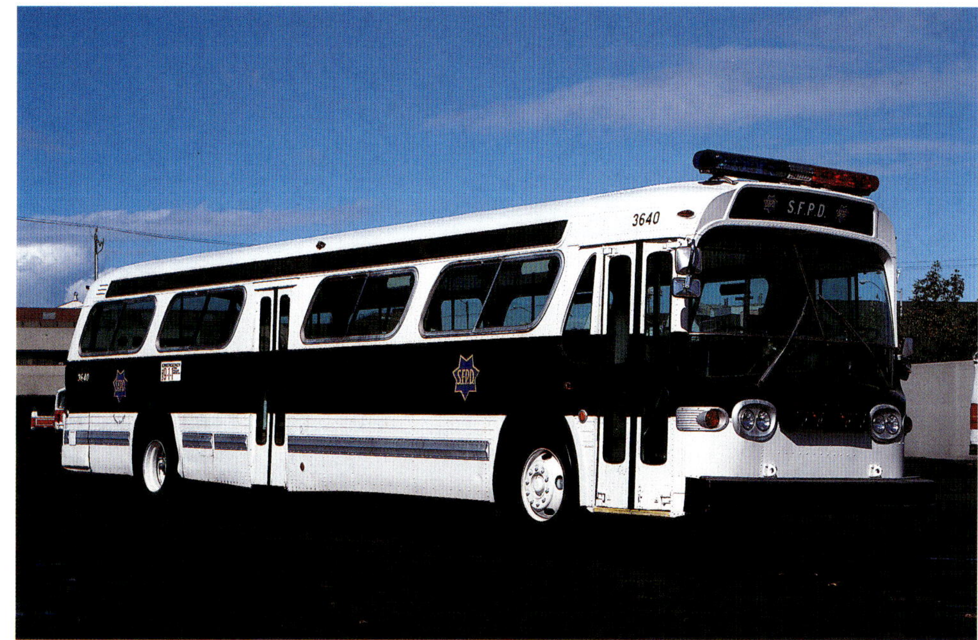

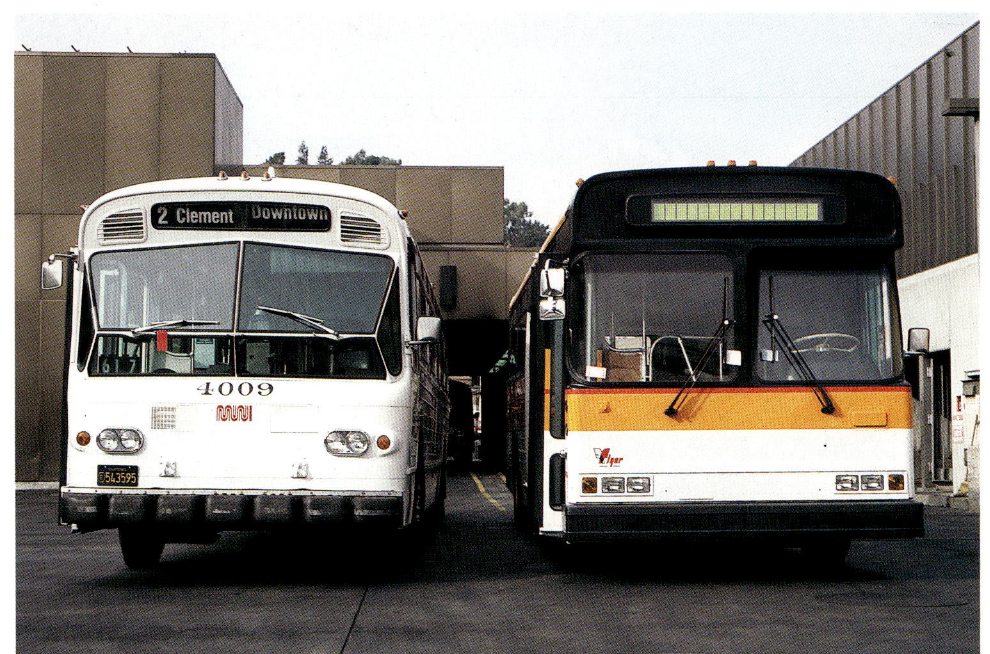

Posed together at Woods Division on February 5, 1985, is Muni's Flexible coach No. 4009, on the left, with a Flyer demonstrator that was temporarily assigned the number 4680 during its testing period.

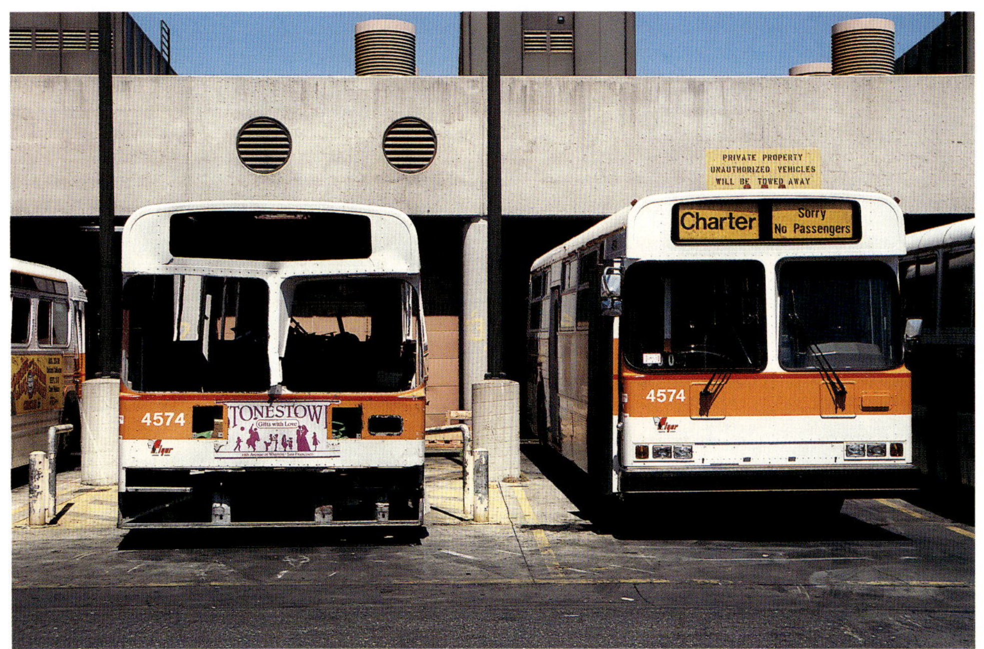

Seeing double? Coaches No. 4574 sit side-by-side at the Woods Division body shop on August 17, 1988; the original No. 4574, on the left, was heavily damaged while being delivered to Muni, so a replacement coach was constructed to fill the void. The original coach was then purchased at salvage value and was eventually stripped of all usable parts prior to being scrapped.

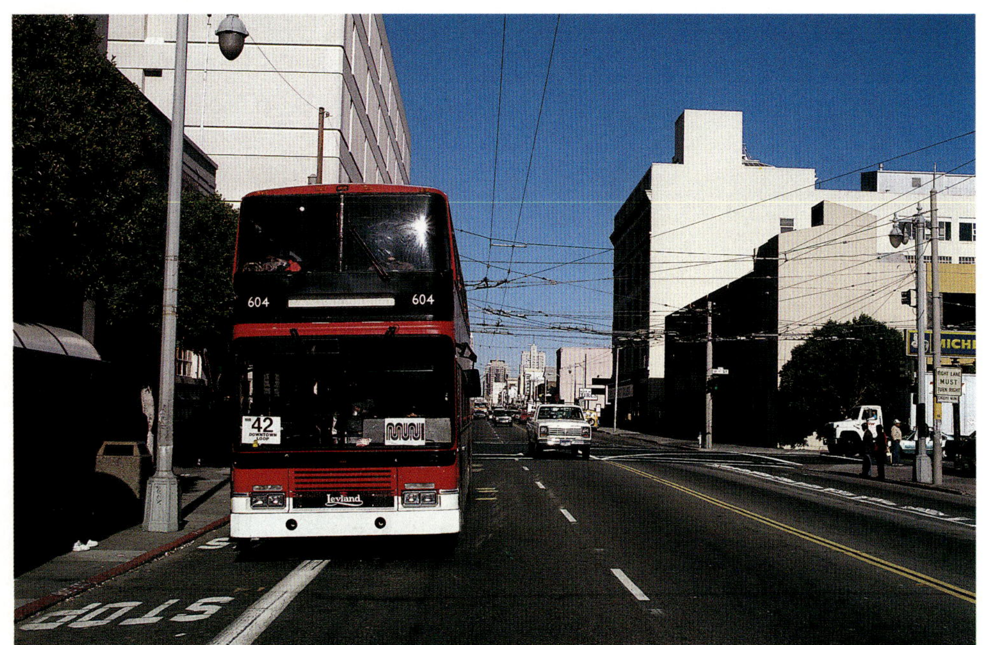

The Municipal Railway leased this double-deck coach from San Francisco tour bus operator Gray Line, to evaluate the performance characteristics of such vehicles in urban transit service. Here, bus No. 604 is photographed southbound on Mission Street, at 11th Street, on February 14, 1990, while serving the patrons of Muni line No. 42.

For a brief period of time this cut-down Mack bus, modified at Muni's 24th & Utah Shop, served patrons of Coit Tower line No. 39. Seen in this photo at the Woods Division, in March 1979, the coach has been preserved as part of the Municipal Railway historical vehicle collection.

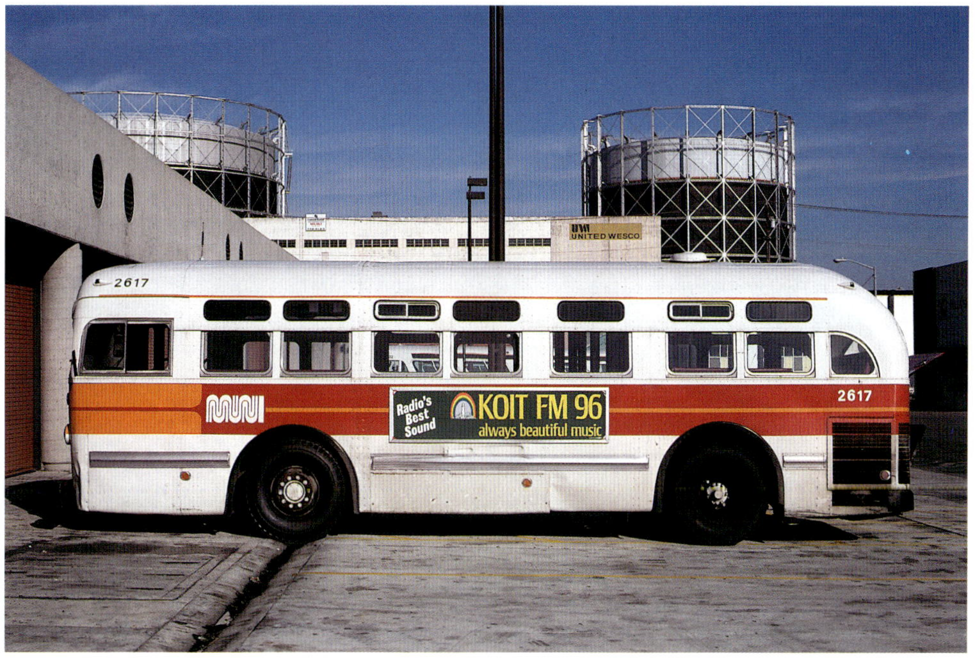

Suffering a severe shortage of serviceable motor coaches, the Municipal Railway purchased a large number of used buses from the Southern California Rapid Transit District in late 1981. One of those vehicles, yet to be renumbered, sits next to Muni's rubber-tired cable car No. 62, at the Woods Division, on November 9, 1981.

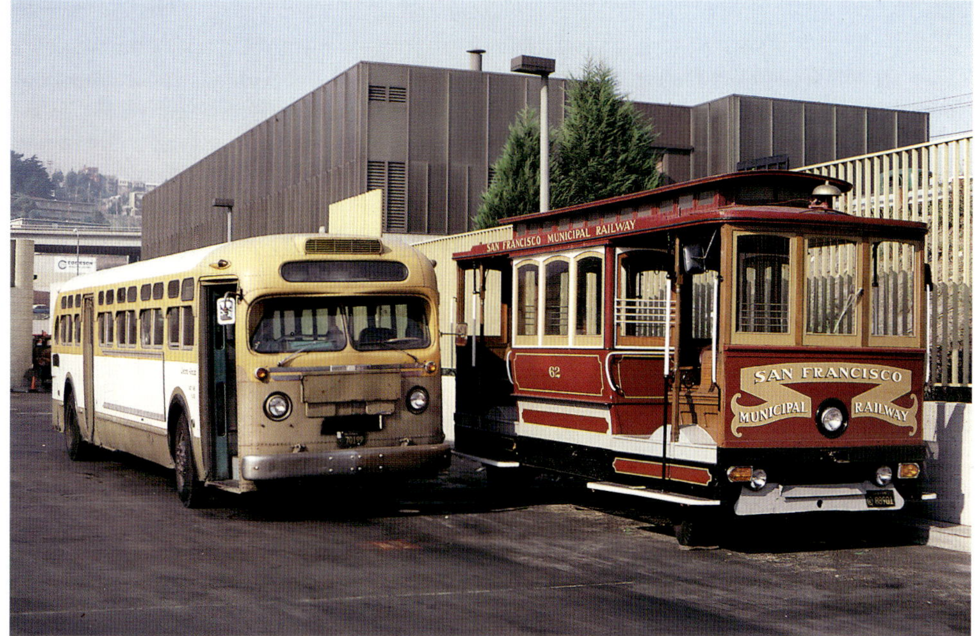

The least successful motor coaches in the city's history were the 25 Grumman/Flexible model 870 buses delivered to the Muni in early 1980. It seemed as if the red hold tags, shown on the window wipers on coach No. 4036 at Woods Division in April 1980, were more often on than off. After a brief sojourn as Muni vehicles, all 25 of the coaches were disposed of to a used bus dealer-- to the everlasting joy of Municipal Railway shop personnel.

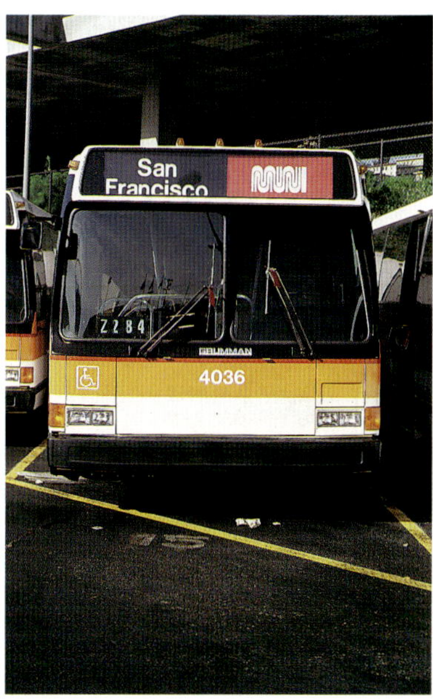

5

MUNI PEOPLE

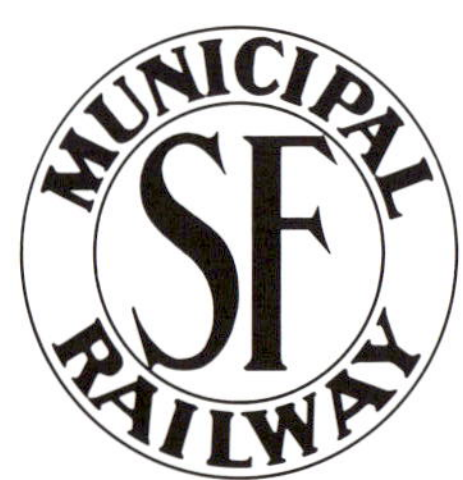

Although in previous chapters we have depicted some of the interesting physical assets of San Francisco's Municipal Railway, there could not be any operation, or maintenance, of those properties without the participation of the various employees that constitute the Muni team that keeps it functioning on a day-to-day basis.

While there are many Municipal Railway employees that perhaps think of their employment as a necessary means toward earning a living, there are a large number of workers that take a genuine extra-curricular interest in the purpose of the railway and its functions. The fact that San Francisco's local transit system operates fleets of streetcars and cable cars has brought numerous railfans and transit fans to the ranks of Muni employees. The cable car operations attract many artisans and craftsmen that take pride in keeping that particular realm of the Municipal Railway in operating order.

Within the pages of this brief chapter are photographs of a few of the interesting individuals that I have been privileged to work with during the years of my Muni employment. Each of these people have added their special qualities to make the San Francisco Municipal Railway an interesting place to work.

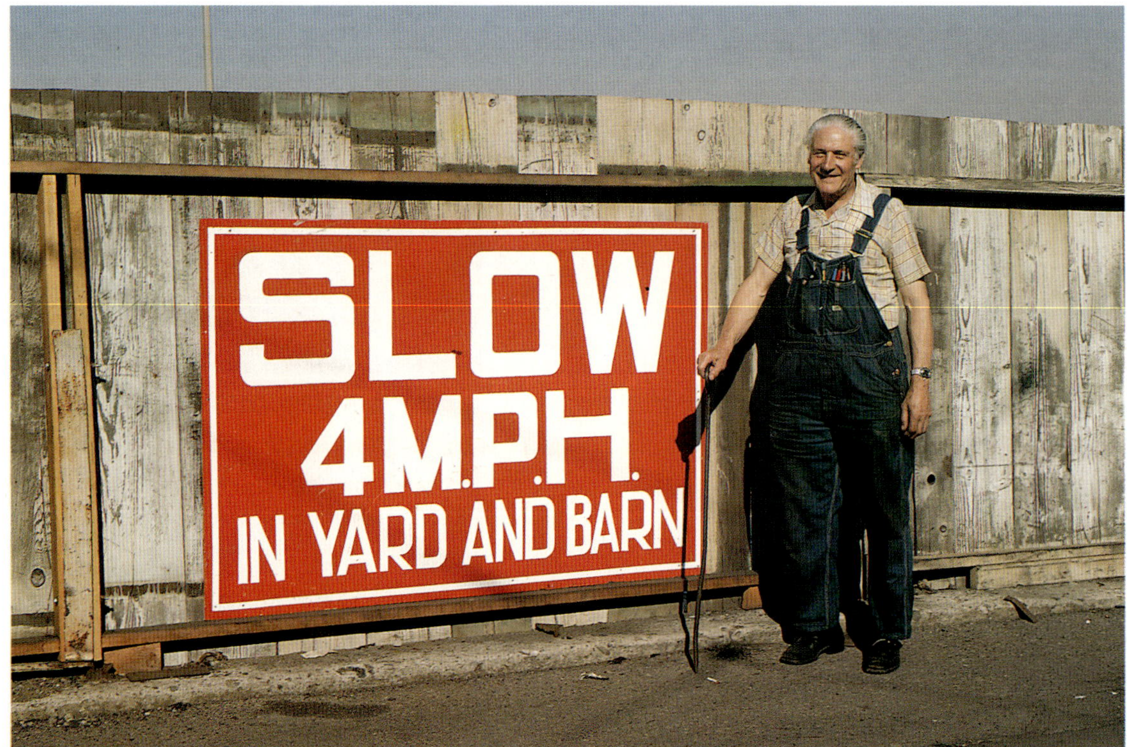

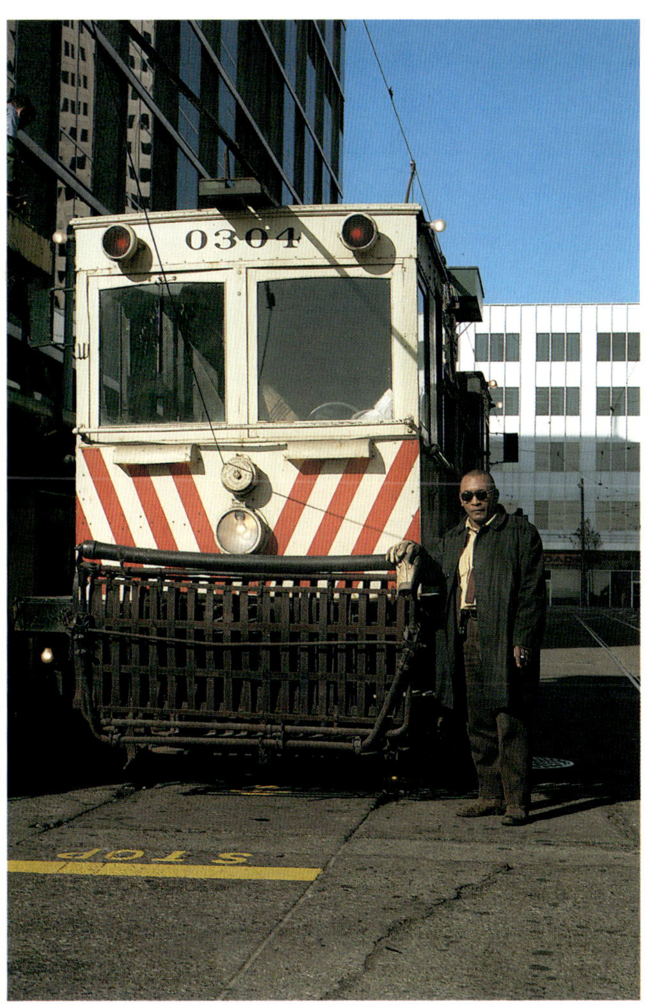

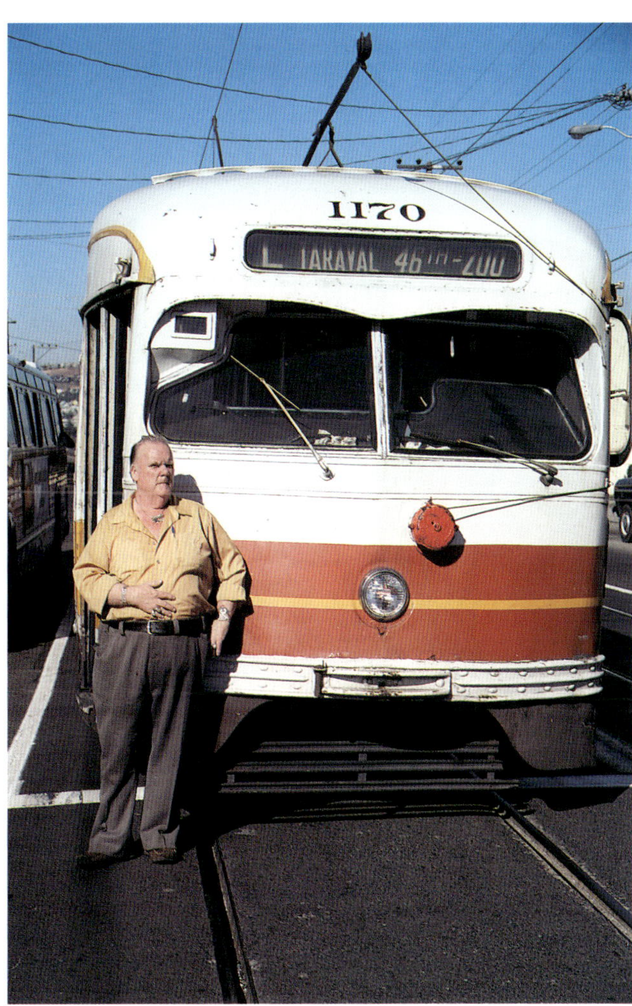

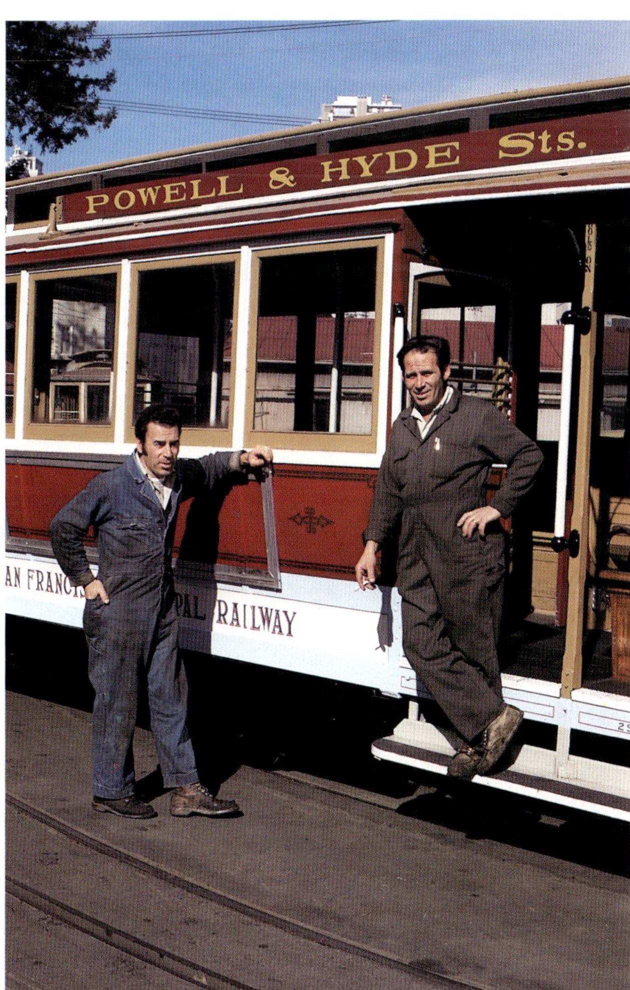

(LEFT) Smiling his usual friendly greeting, the late John Klobucar, switch-iron in hand, poses in Geneva Yard during November 1974. For many years John was a familiar sight as he assigned and dispatched streetcars from that venerable facility.

(ABOVE LEFT) Motorman Jack Smith is one of the Municipal Railway's employees that combines both his vocational and avocational interests into one career. As both gripman and motorman, Jack has proven to be one of Muni's most popular rail-oriented people. Here we see Jack when he was assigned to operate line car No. 0304, and while both vehicle and operator rested at the 11th Street spur track on December 13, 1974.

(ABOVE RIGHT) The late Joe Shook, shown with car No. 1170 on September 22, 1980, was one of the most flamboyant of Muni's motormen during his long, colorful career.

(RIGHT) Two of the skilled workers dedicated to keeping Muni's venerable fleet of vintage cable cars in top operating condition are brothers George (on the left) and Jim Muscat. Hailing originally from the far-off island nation of Malta, these siblings are now among the ranks of senior Municipal Railway cable car shopmen.

6

THE TROLLEY FESTIVAL

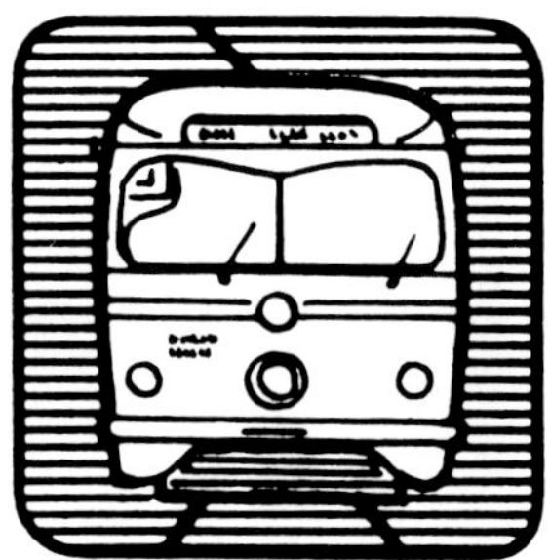

San Francisco has long been regarded as one of the leaders of America's somewhat recent historic preservation movement. Chief among its early accomplishments in that vein were the saving of hundreds of Victorian-era structures from demolition in the immediate post-war era of the late 1940's and the 1950's, and the nation's first successful conversion of a surplus industrial facility into a fashionable shopping complex (The popular Ghirardelli Square development.).

And when it came time to entirely close down the city's main tourist attraction, the venerable cable railway system, for a complete rebuilding in the years 1982-1984, a group of influential trolley enthusiasts took the initiative and formulated a plan that persuaded local merchants, politicians, and officials of the San Francisco Municipal Railway, that the establishment of an historic trolley festival—with vehicles from around the world participating—could be a potential replacement attraction for the sidelined cable cars.

Thus was born the concept of the now-famous San Francisco Historic Trolley Festival. First operated during the summer of 1983, the festival continued as an annual summertime event, even after the cable car system was reopened in 1984, until the fall of 1987. Although the trolley festival was considered more of a good-will, than financial, success, plans have been made to incorporate the operation of vintage trolley cars as a regular part of year-round Municipal Railway operations upon completion of the upper Market Street rebuilding project and construction of the new Embarcadero Parkway.

Though it has not operated on a regular basis since the Loma Prieta earthquake of October 17, 1989, due to a need to channel city funds to earthquake repair projects, several "mini" trolley festivals have been operated on certain long holiday weekends, or for specific special occasions. A highly-vocal local support group, known as the Market Street Railway Company, has maintained constant pressure on local politicians, and the Municipal Railway, in order to help keep the trolley festival movement alive. Through their efforts, in addition, several vintage transit vehicles are being restored and maintained at the festival's Mint Yard, located at Market Street and Duboce Avenue.

Here, then, are a selection of photographs that depict the Trolley Festival as it appeared during the initial years of its operation. Many of the cars shown have been returned to their regular homes, and were utilized for only one particular year's festival at a time when Muni was rounding up its own vintage fleet. Now that the Municipal Railway actually owns its own roster of historic tram cars, it is highly unlikely that there will be a requirement to rent or borrow any additional vehicles in the foreseeable future.

It should be noted, that in addition to its fleet of vintage streetcars, the San Francisco Municipal Railway also owns and maintains a number of historic trolley coaches and motor buses; these are frequently used in conjunction with the operation of the Trolley Festival, or at times when a representative Muni vehicle is needed to make an appearance in a parade or other civic activity.

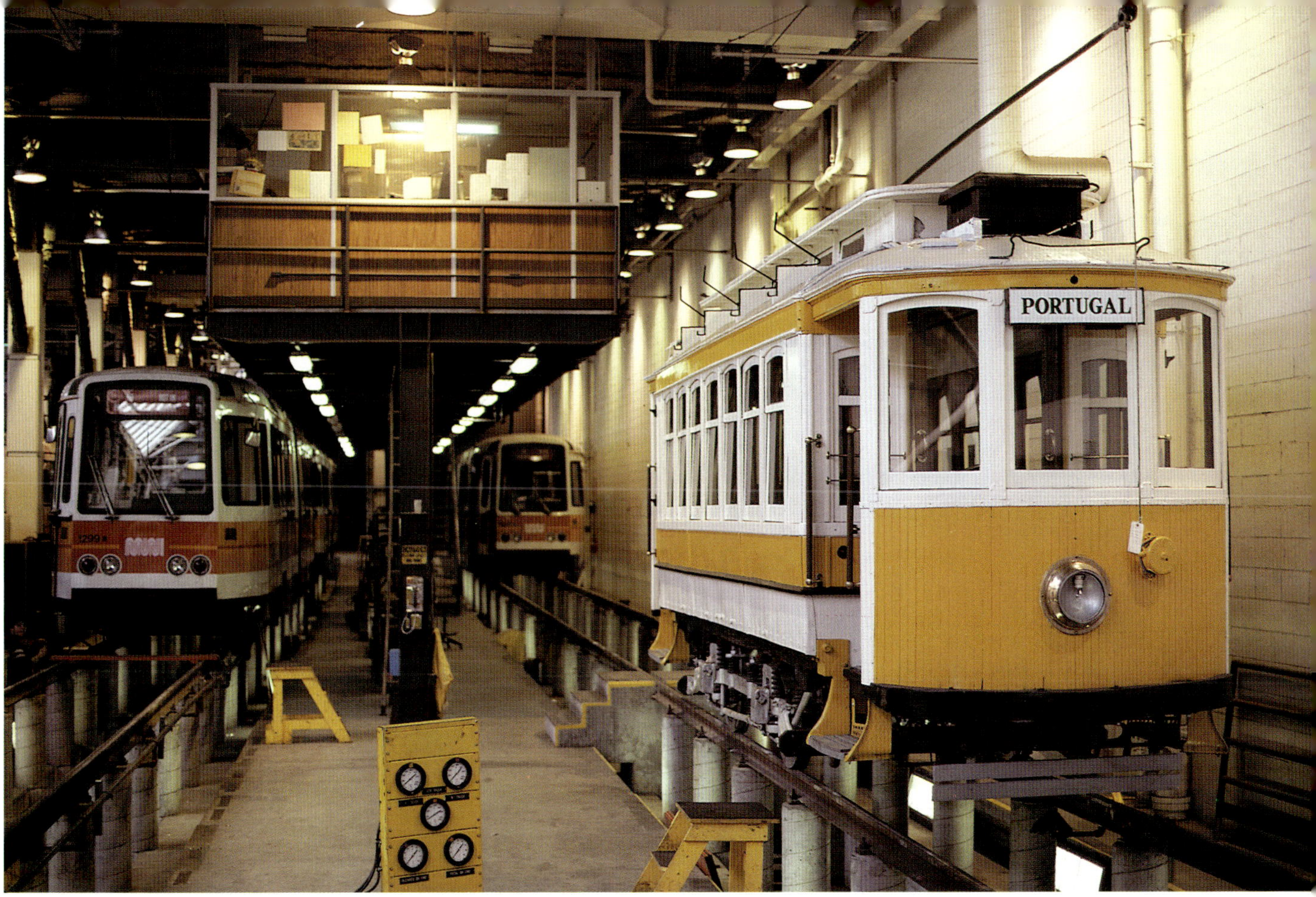

(ABOVE) The first operable non-Muni item of rolling stock to arrive for service in the initial San Francisco Historic Trolley Festival was car No. 122 from far-off Oporto, Portugal, by way of Glenwood, Oregon. Shown here, on June 12, 1983, while being inspected on Metro Center's running repair pit, the recently-painted car has yet to have its numbers affixed.

(BELOW) Running mate to No. 122 was another Oporto car, No. 189, shown southbound on Market Street, at Powell Street, on July 10, 1983. This car, wearing its original brown livery, was eventually purchased by the Muni and repainted a bright red hue.

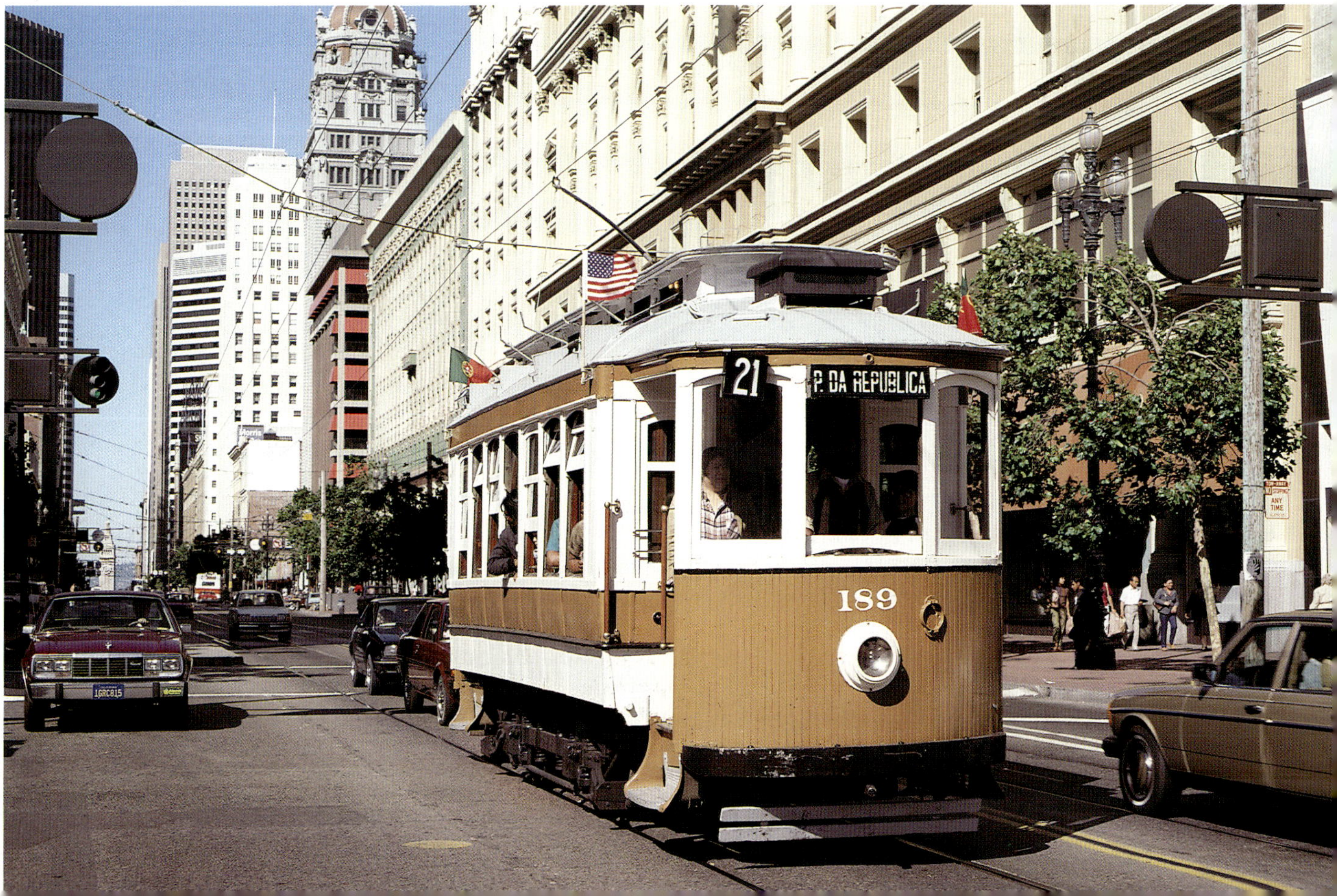

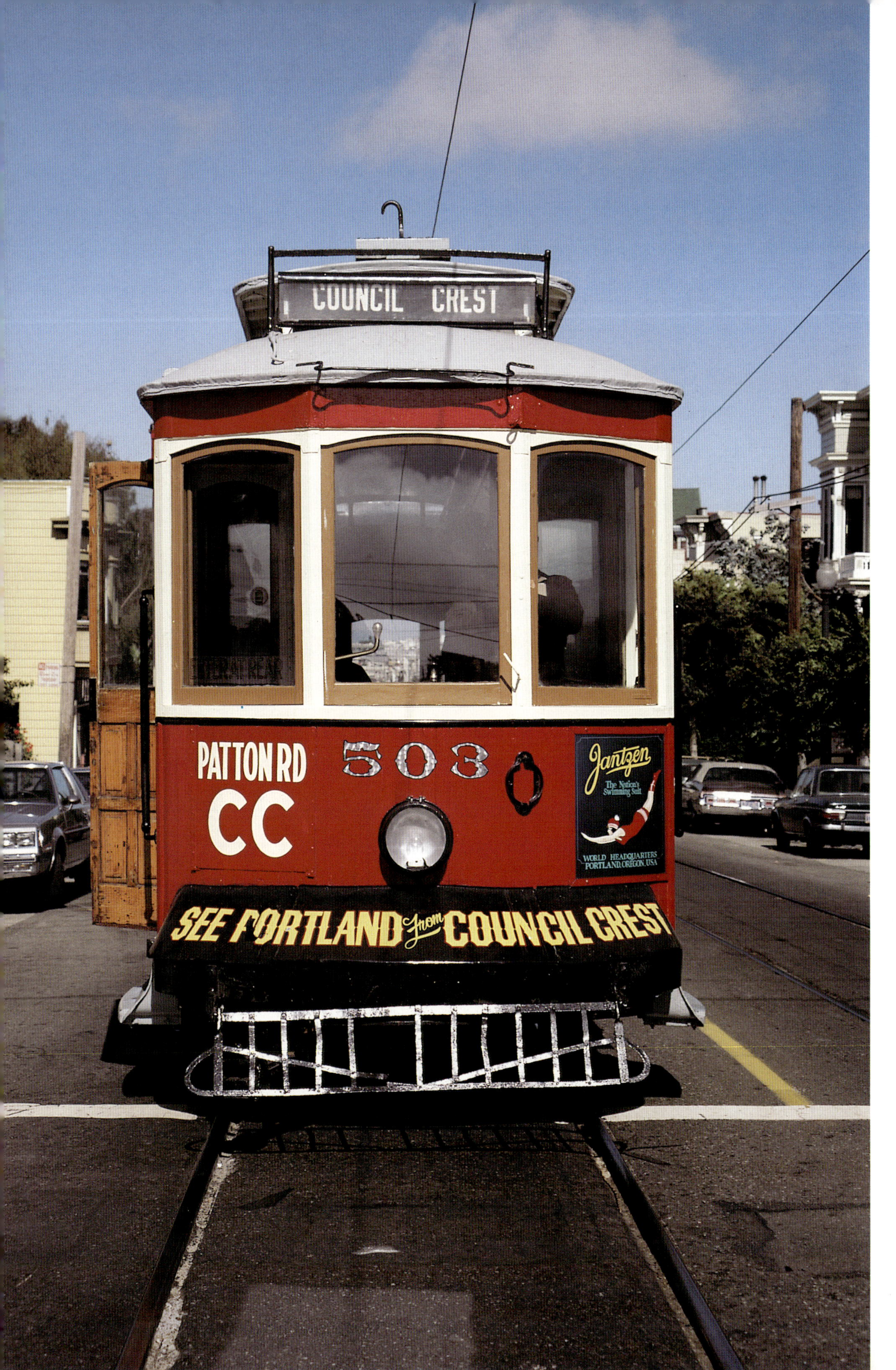
COUNCIL CREST
PATTON RD
CC
503
Jantzen
The Nation's Swimming Suit
WORLD HEADQUARTERS
PORTLAND, OREGON, USA
SEE PORTLAND from COUNCIL CREST

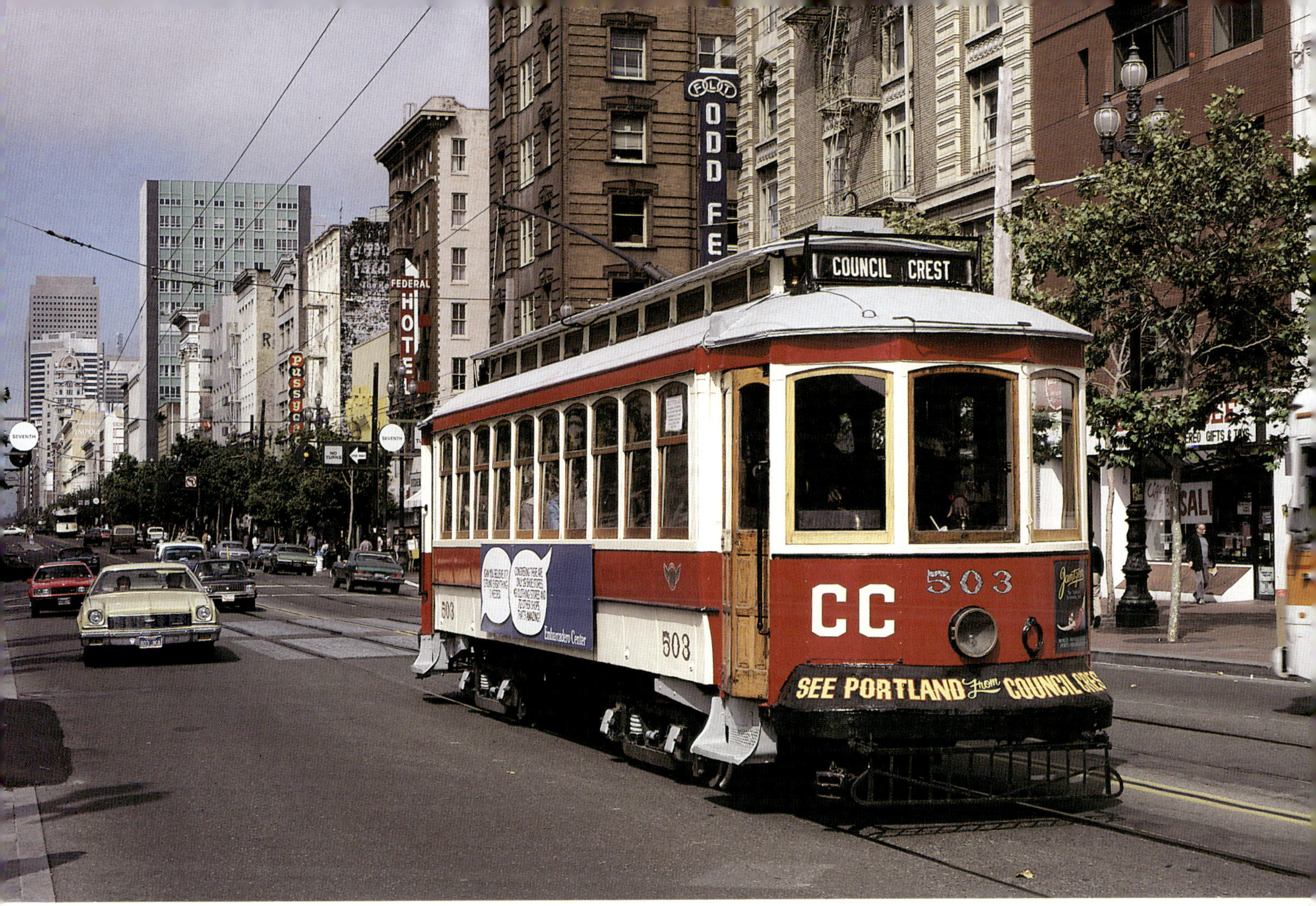

(OPPOSITE PAGE) Arguably the finest car of its vintage in the Trolley Festival, was car No. 503--formerly of the Portland Traction Company. Shown here as it sits on 17th Street, on July 28, 1983, the vehicle's classic lines and interesting paint scheme recall those wonderful days when this car operated to Portland's Council Crest neighborhood.

(ABOVE) Though on static display for a number of years at a Boy Scout camp, car No. 503 was made operational once again by the addition of trucks, motors, and controls, from Melbourne, Australia. Here the car is shown southbound on Market Street, at 7th Street, on July 24, 1983.

(RIGHT) Speaking of Melbourne, here's former Melbourne Tramways No. 648 waiting at the passenger island outbound on Market Street, at Van Ness Avenue, on July 4, 1983.

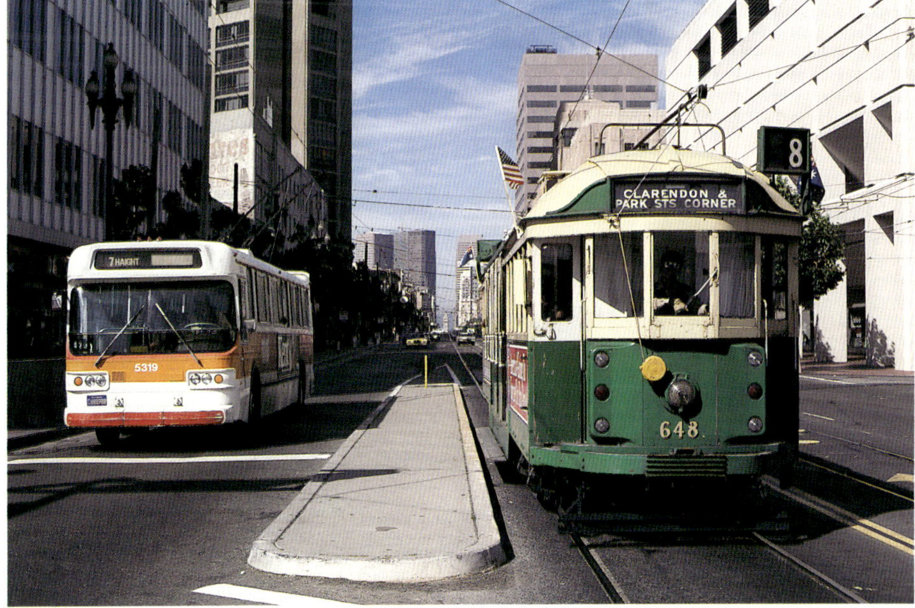

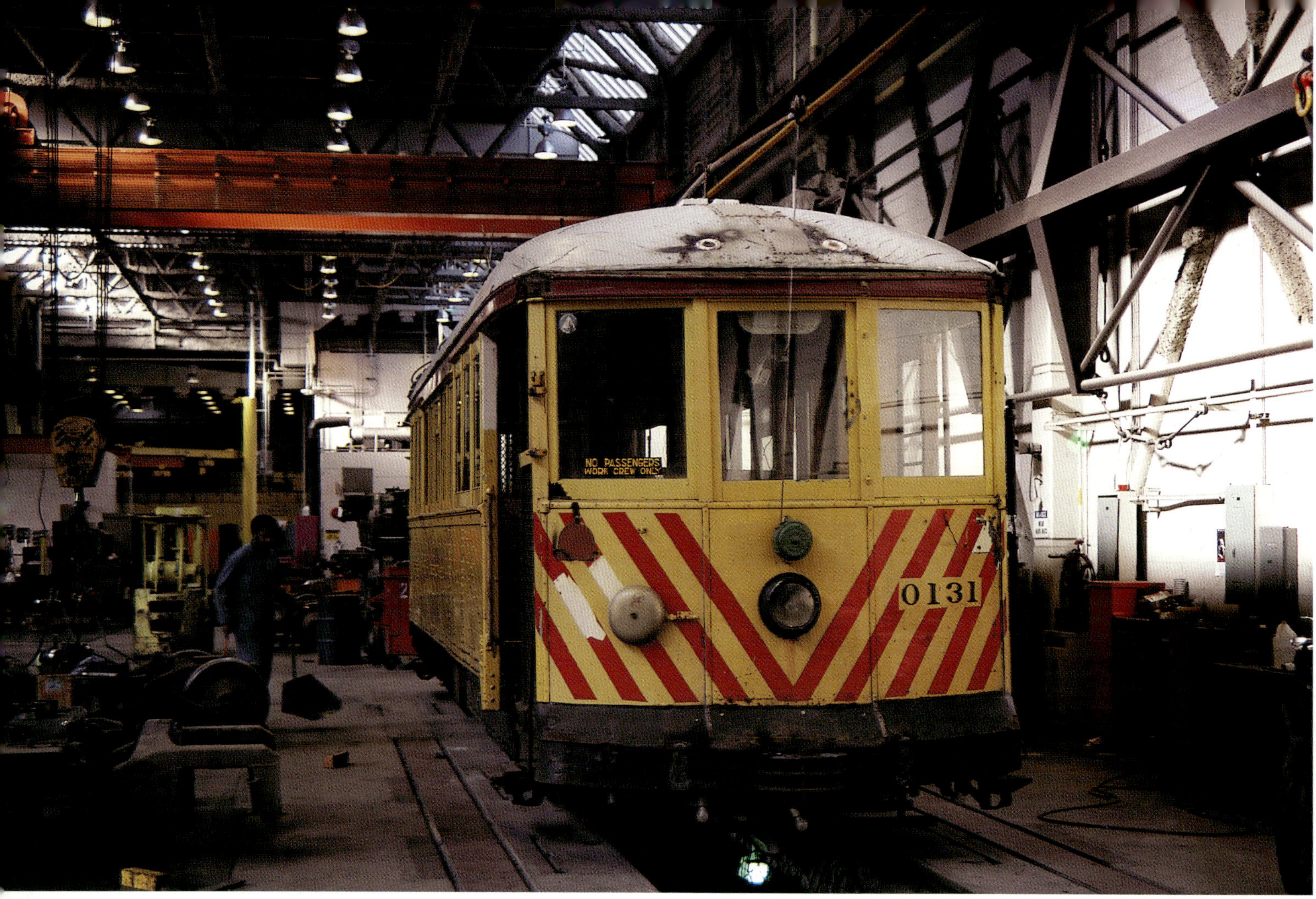

NO PASSENGERS
WORK CREW ONLY
0131

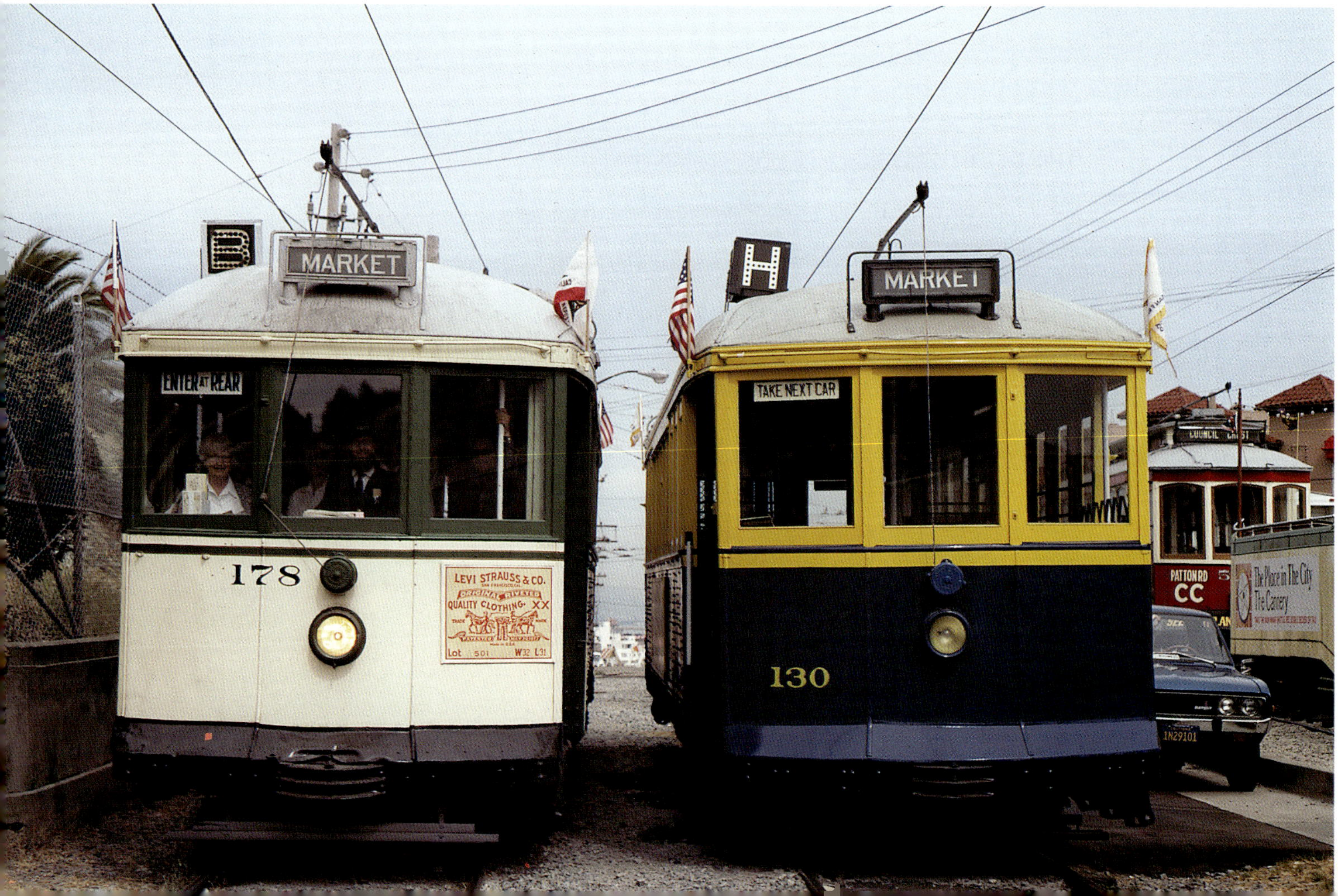

B
MARKET
ENTER AT REAR
178
LEVI STRAUSS & CO.
QUALITY CLOTHING
H
MARKET
TAKE NEXT CAR
130
PATTON RD
CC

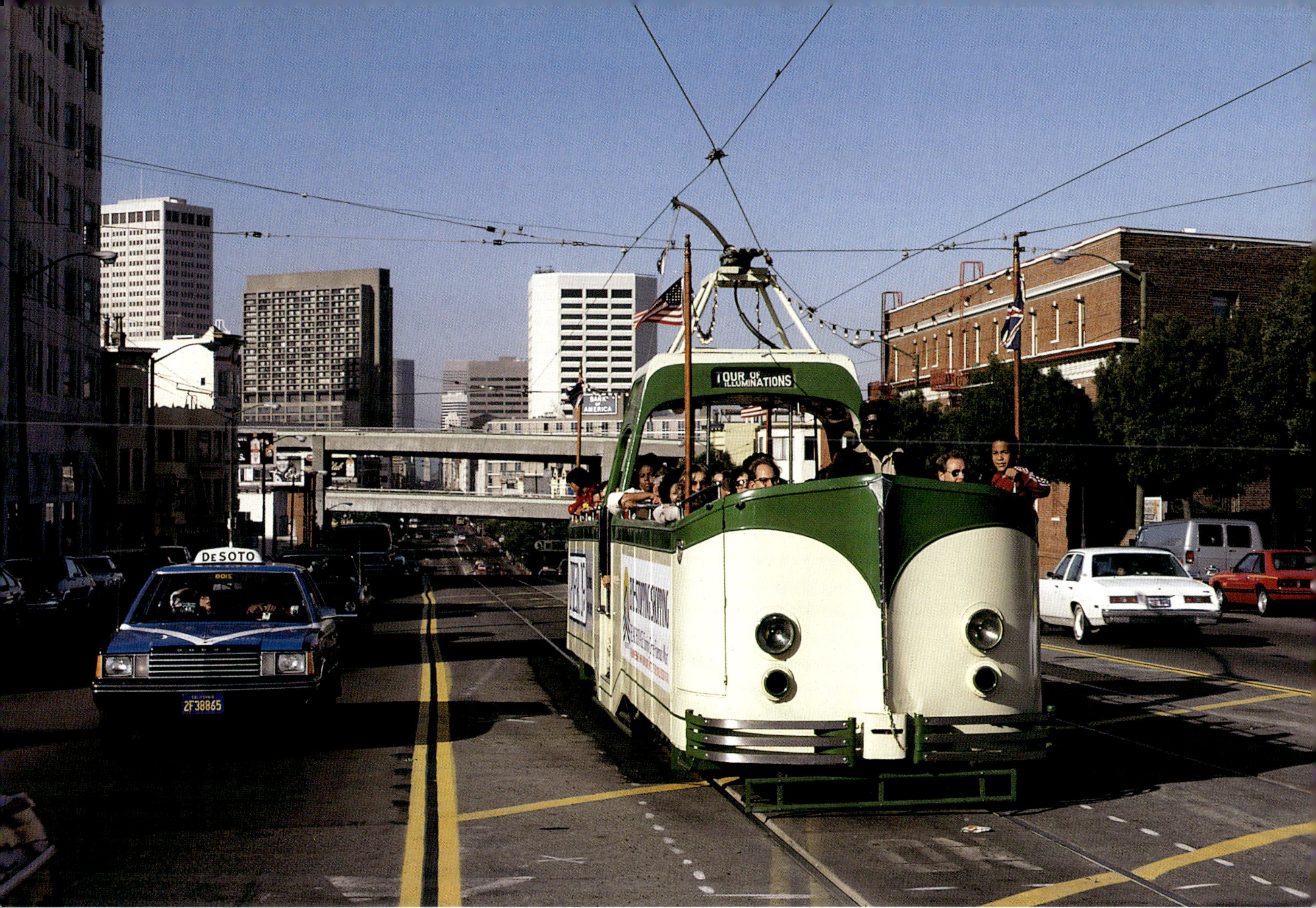

(OPPOSITE TOP) The conversion of former wrecker car No. 0131 back to its prior passenger car configuration, as No. 130, is underway deep within the confines of Muni's Metro Center shop complex in this view recorded on April 5, 1983.

(OPPOSITE BOTTOM) When it finally emerged, resplendent in the Municipal Railway's late-1930's blue and gold paint scheme, car No. 130 became one of the riding public's favorite cars during the initial Trolley Festival. Here, car No. 130 compares its paint job with a later-era Muni color scheme, worn by car No. 178, while parked on the Mint Yard storage track on August 14, 1983.

(ABOVE) Undoubtedly the public's Very Favorite Vehicle during the original Trolley Festival was former Blackpool boat car No. 226, shown here flying its skull-and-cross-bones flag on the trolley rope. Motorman Joe Batiste is bringing yet another load of happy passengers outbound on Market Street, approaching Duboce Avenue, on July 31, 1983.

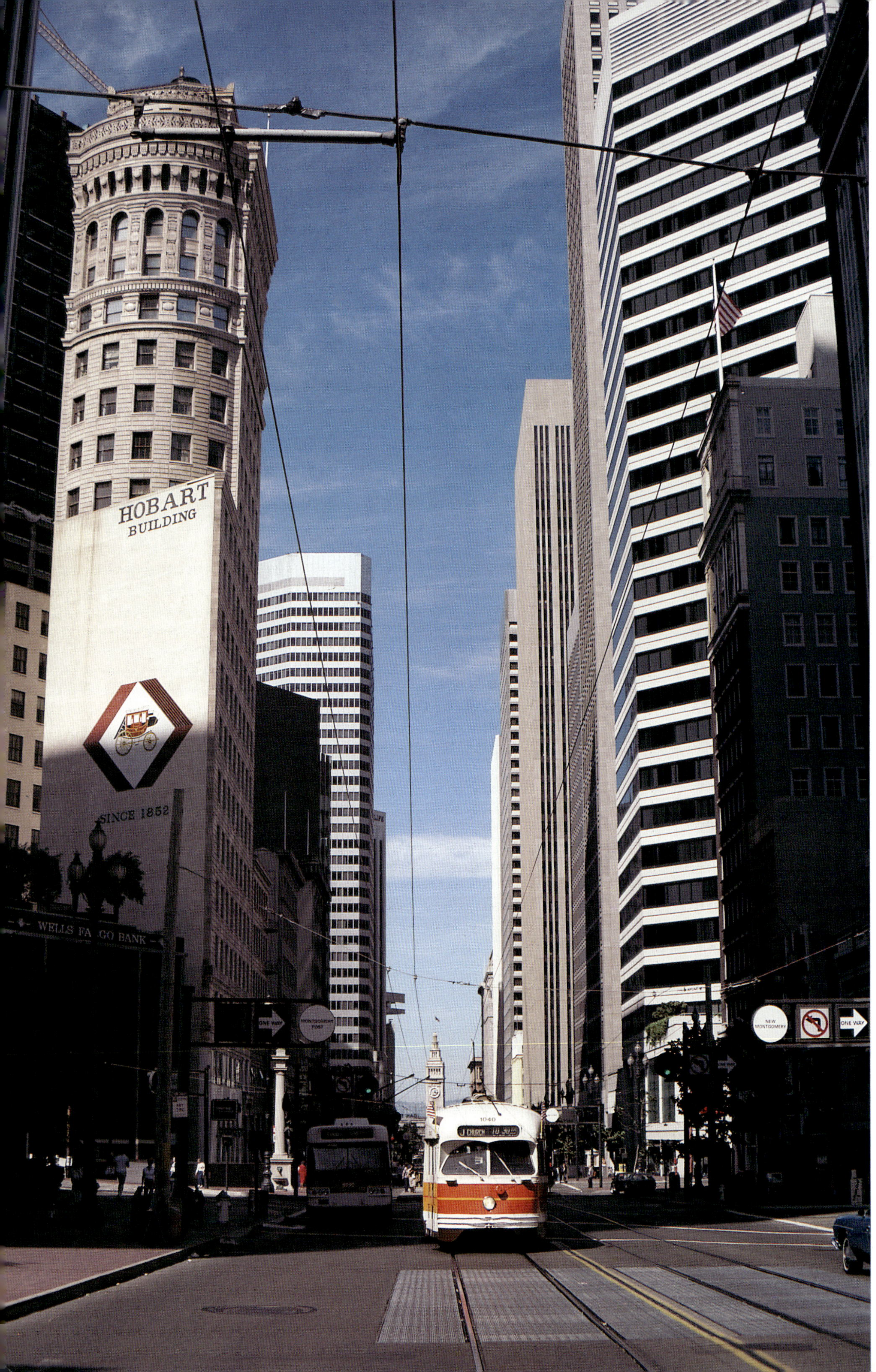
HOBART
BUILDING
SINCE 1852
WELLS FARGO BANK
ONE WAY
ONE WAY

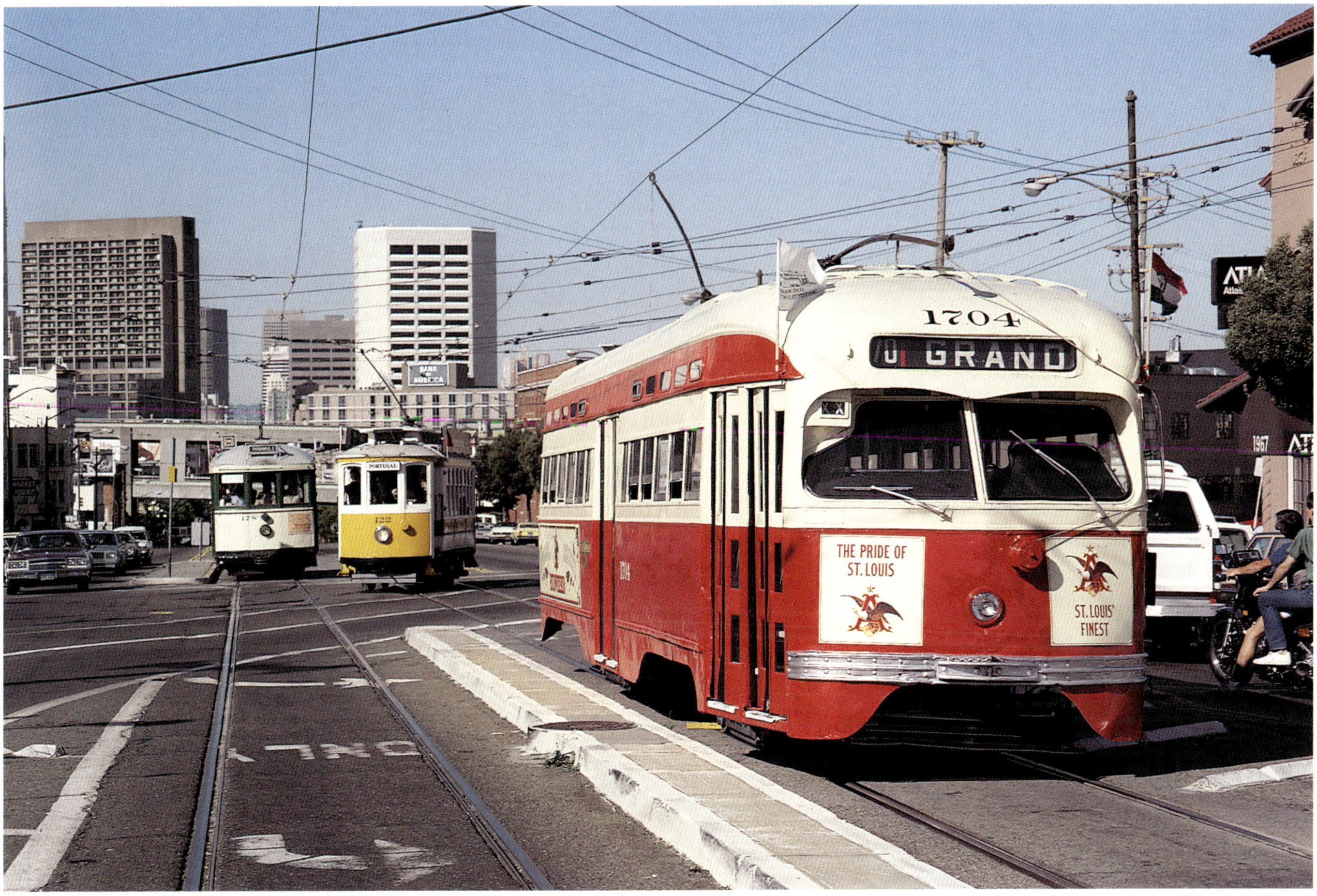

(OPPOSITE PAGE) That the skyline of The City has changed dramatically in recent years is best demonstrated by this view showing P.C.C. car No. 1040 southbound on Market Street, at Montgomery Street, on July 4, 1983. Dwarfing the distant Ferry Building, the city's new high-rise buildings reflect what many have termed the "Manhattanization" of San Francisco.

(ABOVE) Resting upon trackage that is now covered with asphalt, P.C.C. No. 1704, in the livery of the St. Louis Public Service Company, is depicted on July 10, 1983. This reconversion of one of Muni's ex-St. Louis cars into an approximation of its former self, was the railway's initial effort at replicating the paint scheme of another transit property.

(RIGHT) Although it made the long journey out from Wisconsin, former Milwaukee Electric Railway and Transport Company car No. 978 was unable to participate in the Trolley Festival when it was found that years of corrosion had lead to a major structural failure. The car, shown here at Metro Center on July 17, 1983, was eventually returned to its home state to await a date for a thorough rebuilding of its lower carbody.

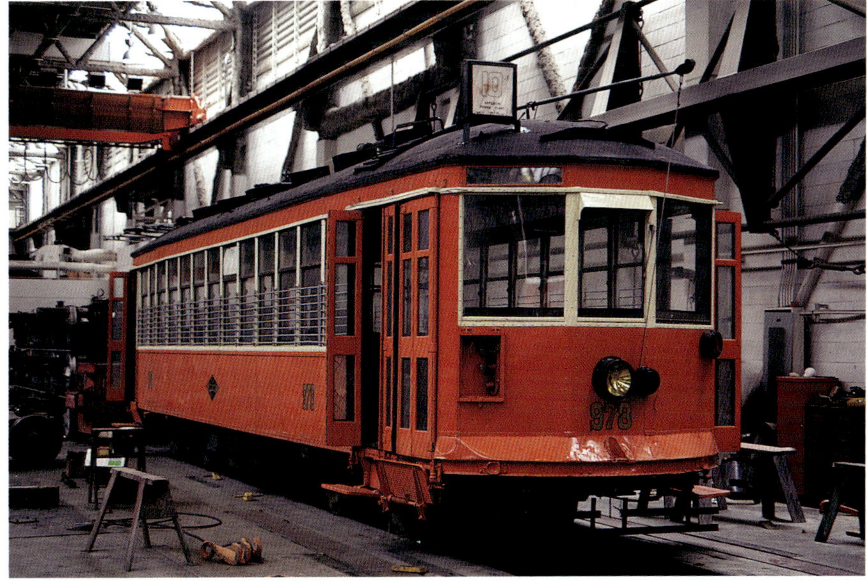

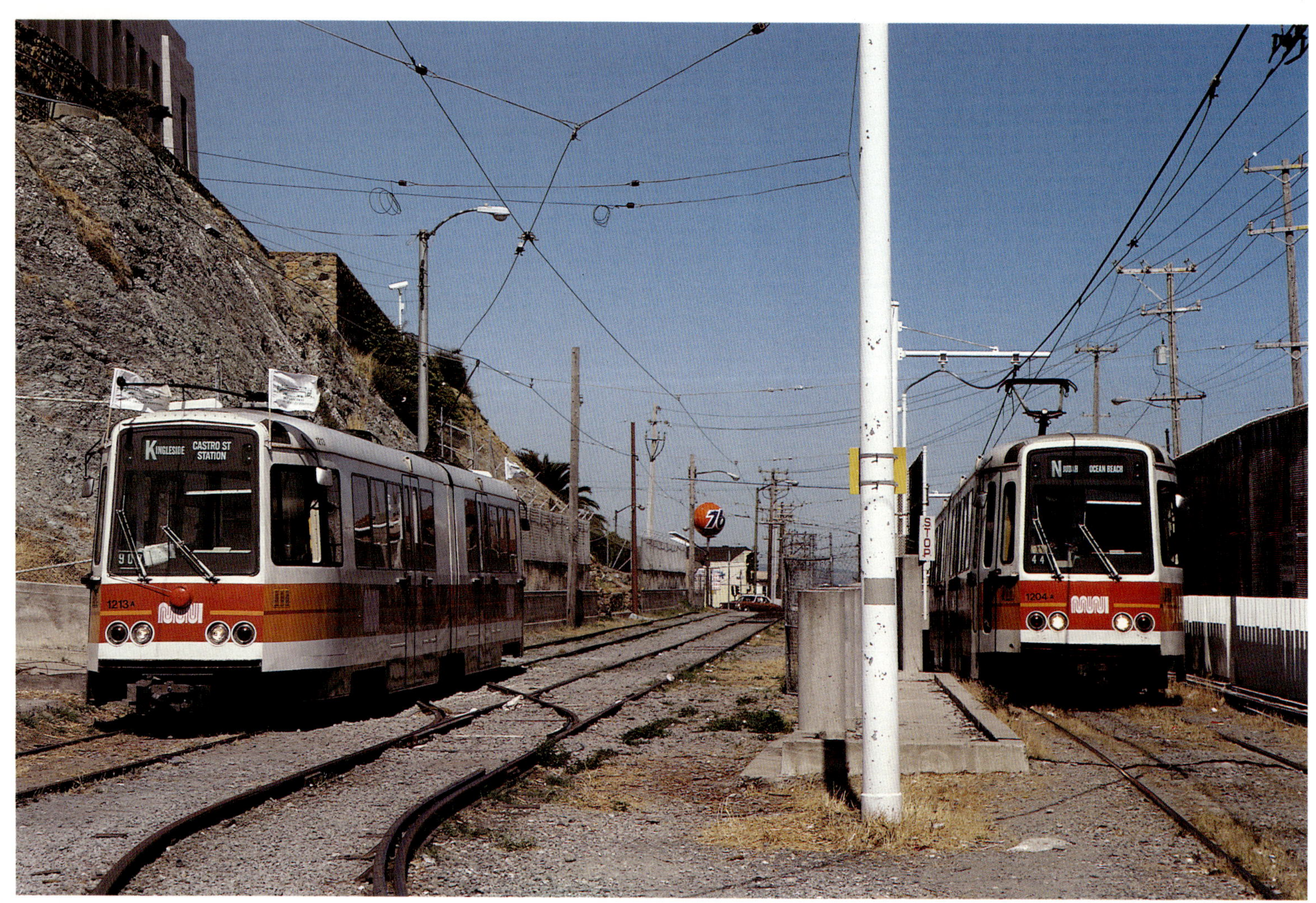

(ABOVE) Operating side-by-side along the former alignment of Duboce Avenue, are L.R.V.s No. 1213, on the left, and No. 1204, on the right. Car No. 1213, in Trolley Festival service, utilizes a trolley pole as its current-collector, while car No. 1204, emerging from the Market Street Subway, is current-collecting with its single-arm pantograph. Both vehicles are westbound on July 3, 1983.

(OPPOSITE TOP) As it approaches Grant Avenue, southbound on Market Street on July 10, 1983, L.R.V. No. 1213 has the street all to itself-- a far cry from normal traffic conditions.

(OPPOSITE BOTTOM) Arriving at the Duboce Avenue passenger island, outbound on Market Street on July 10, 1983, L.R.V. No. 1213 is about to turn west onto the private-right-of-way that it will traverse to busy Church Street.

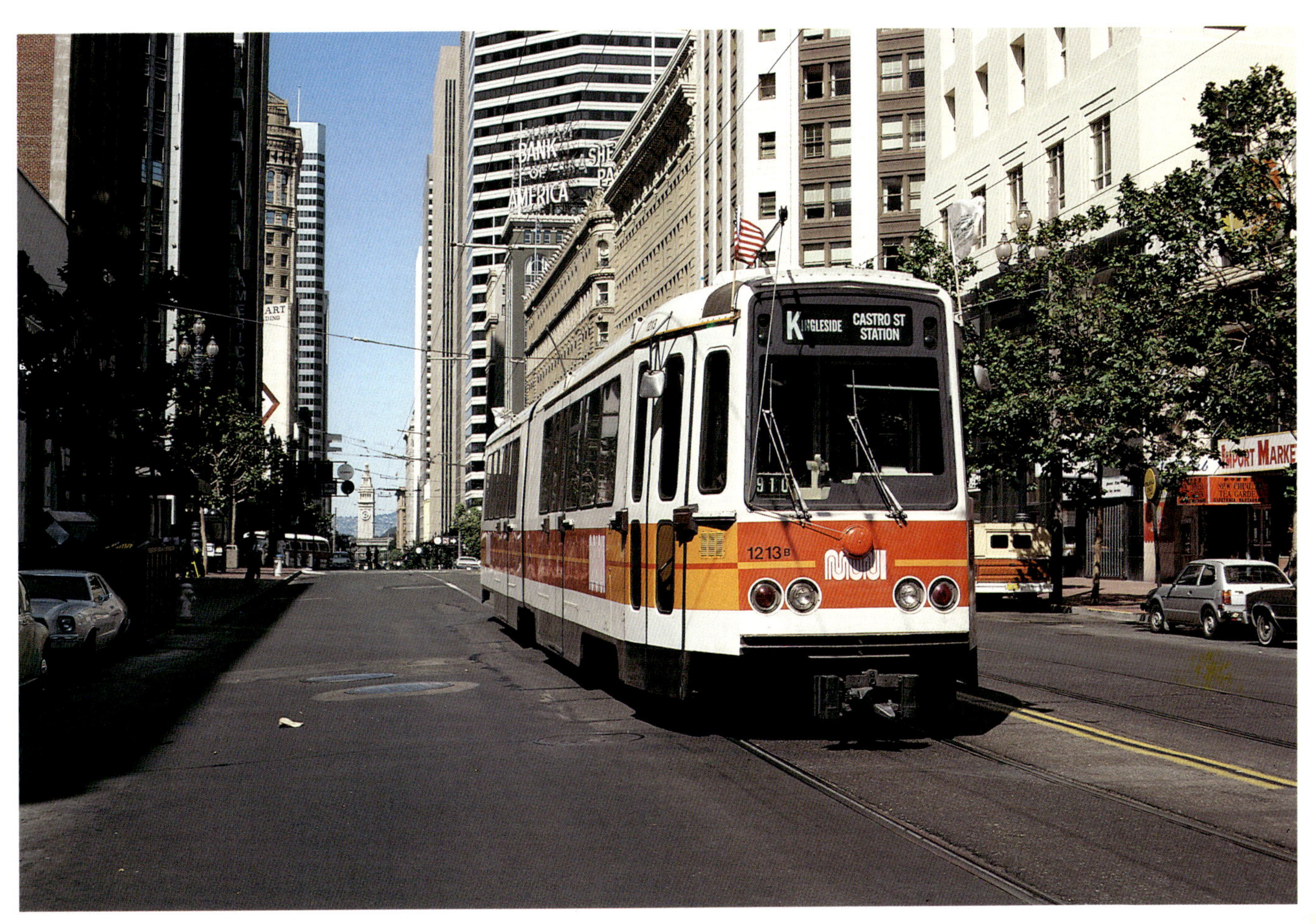

BANK OF AMERICA
K INGLESIDE CASTRO ST STATION
1213 B

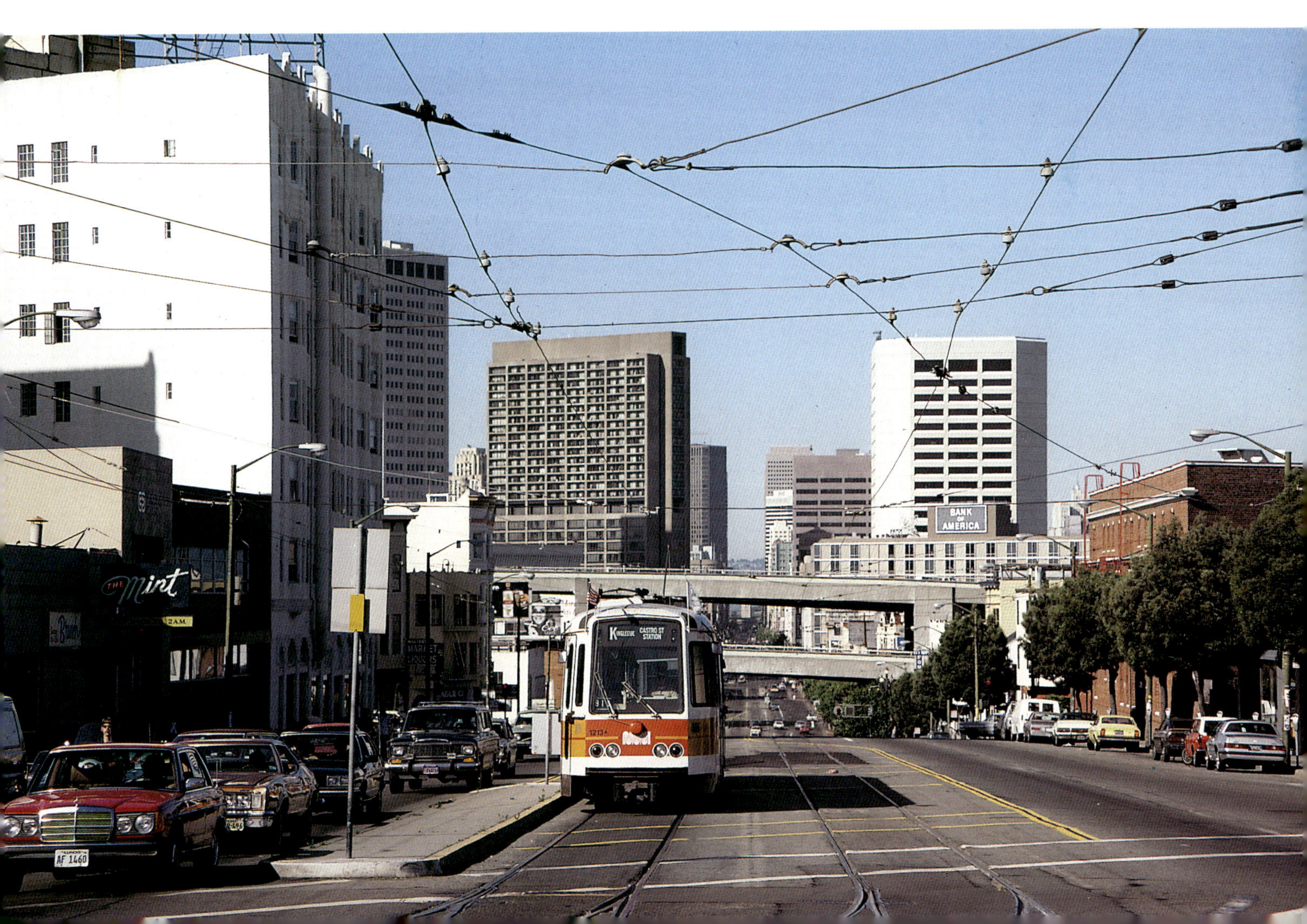

BANK OF AMERICA
K INGLESIDE CASTRO ST STATION
The Mint
2 A.M.
AF 1460

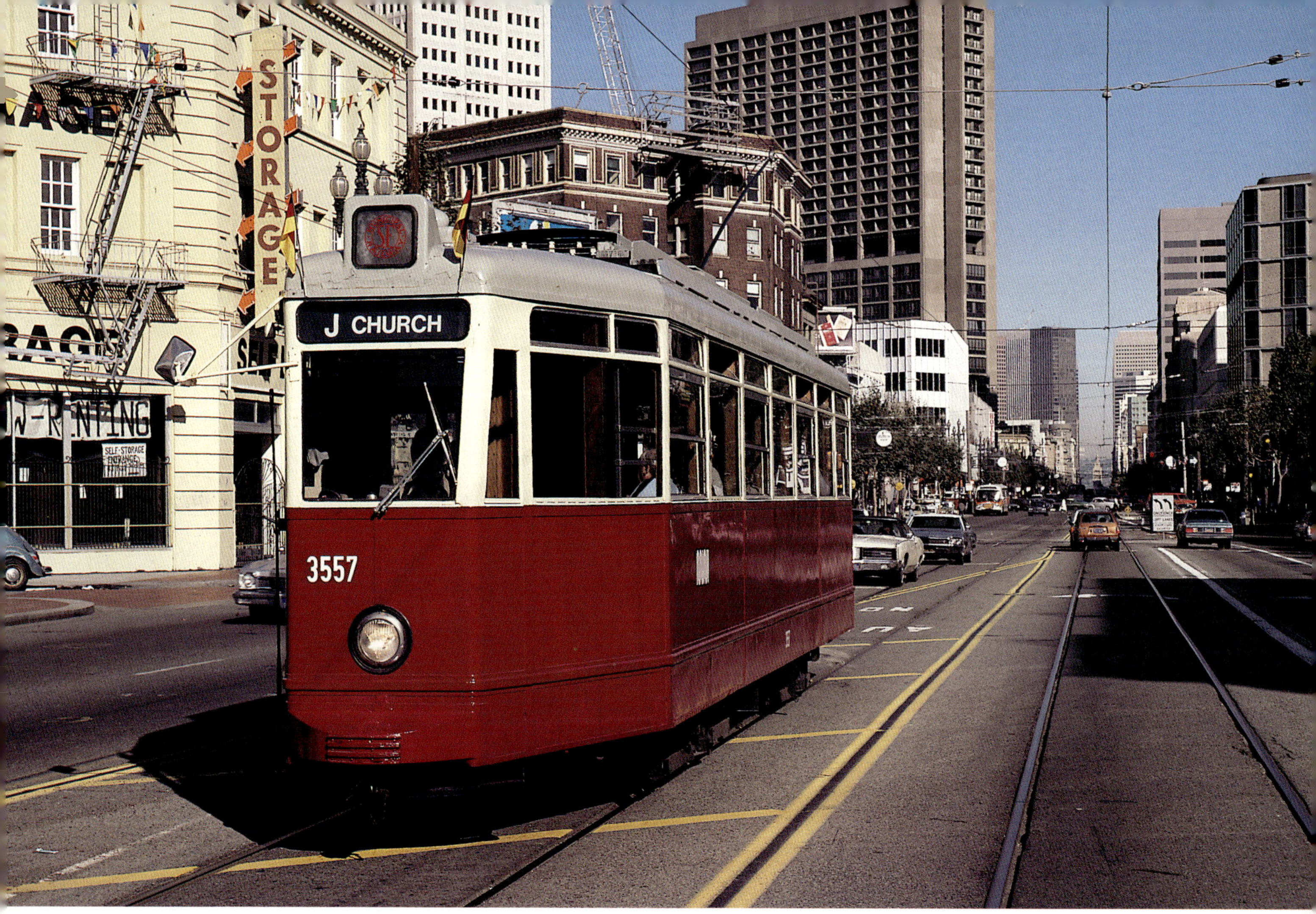

(ABOVE) Germany's contribution to the Historic Trolley Festival is former Hamburg tram car No. 3557, shown outbound on Market Street, approaching Gough Street, on November 27, 1983. This sleek vehicle is one of the most agile of all the festival cars, and one that gives a surprisingly comfortable ride.
(RIGHT) This view of car No. 3557's interior, shows to advantage the large picture windows, as well as the molded, curved-wood seats.

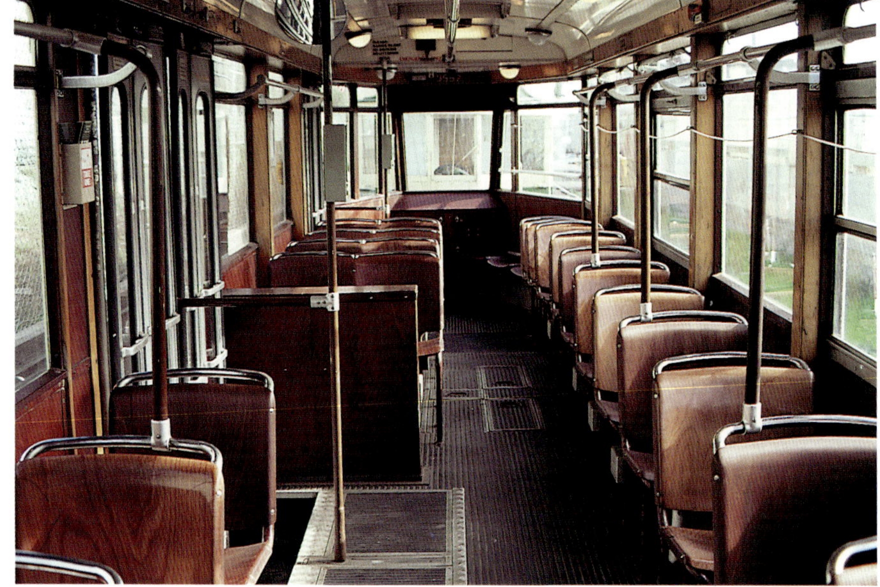

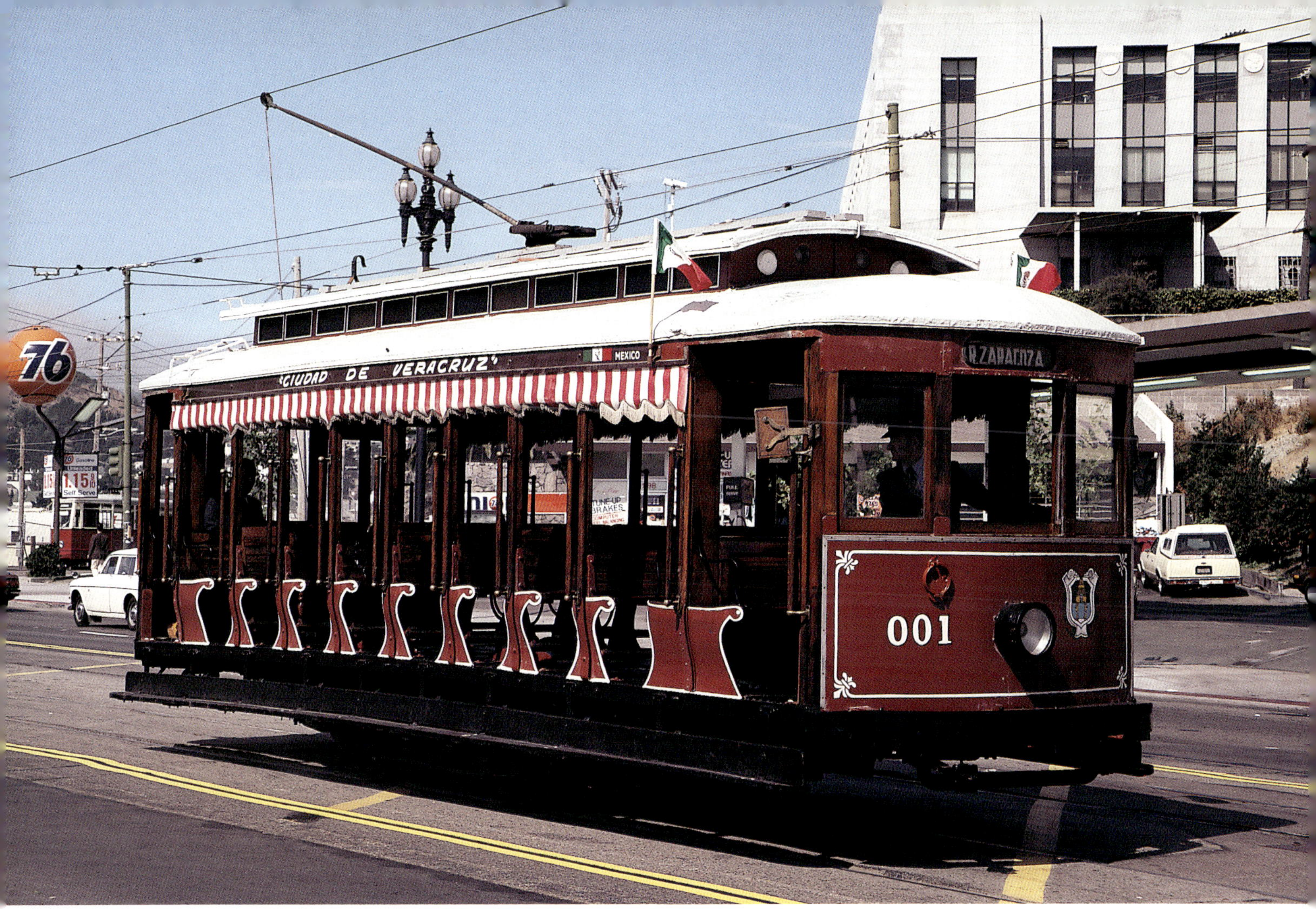

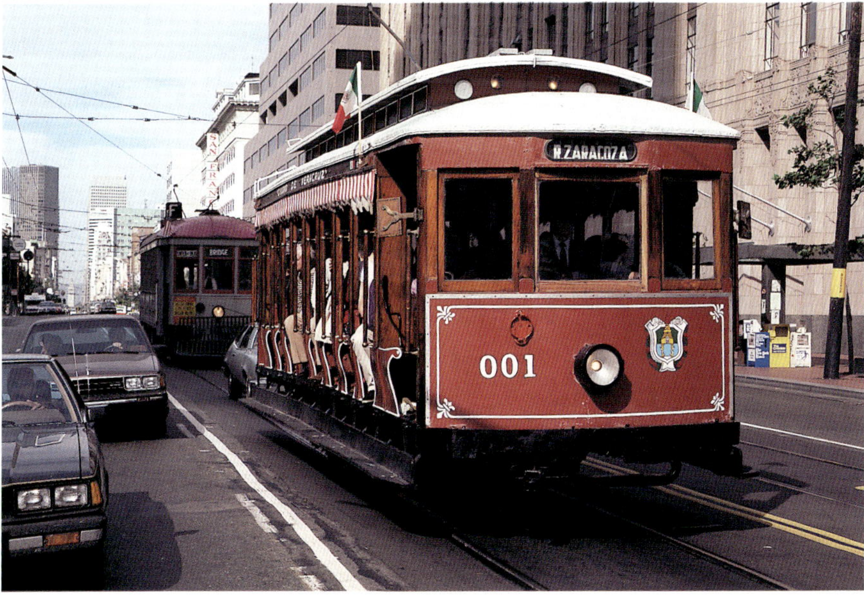

(ABOVE) Adding to the international flavor of the Trolley Festival, car No. 001, loaned by the citizens of Veracruz, Mexico, made its debut in the 1984 operating season. Here we note the car inbound on Market Street, as it leaves Mint Yard for the East Bay Terminal in August 1984.
(LEFT) Used only between the East Bay Terminal and 11th and Market Streets, due to its fragile braking system, car No. 001 is outbound between 9th and 10th Streets with a capacity load.

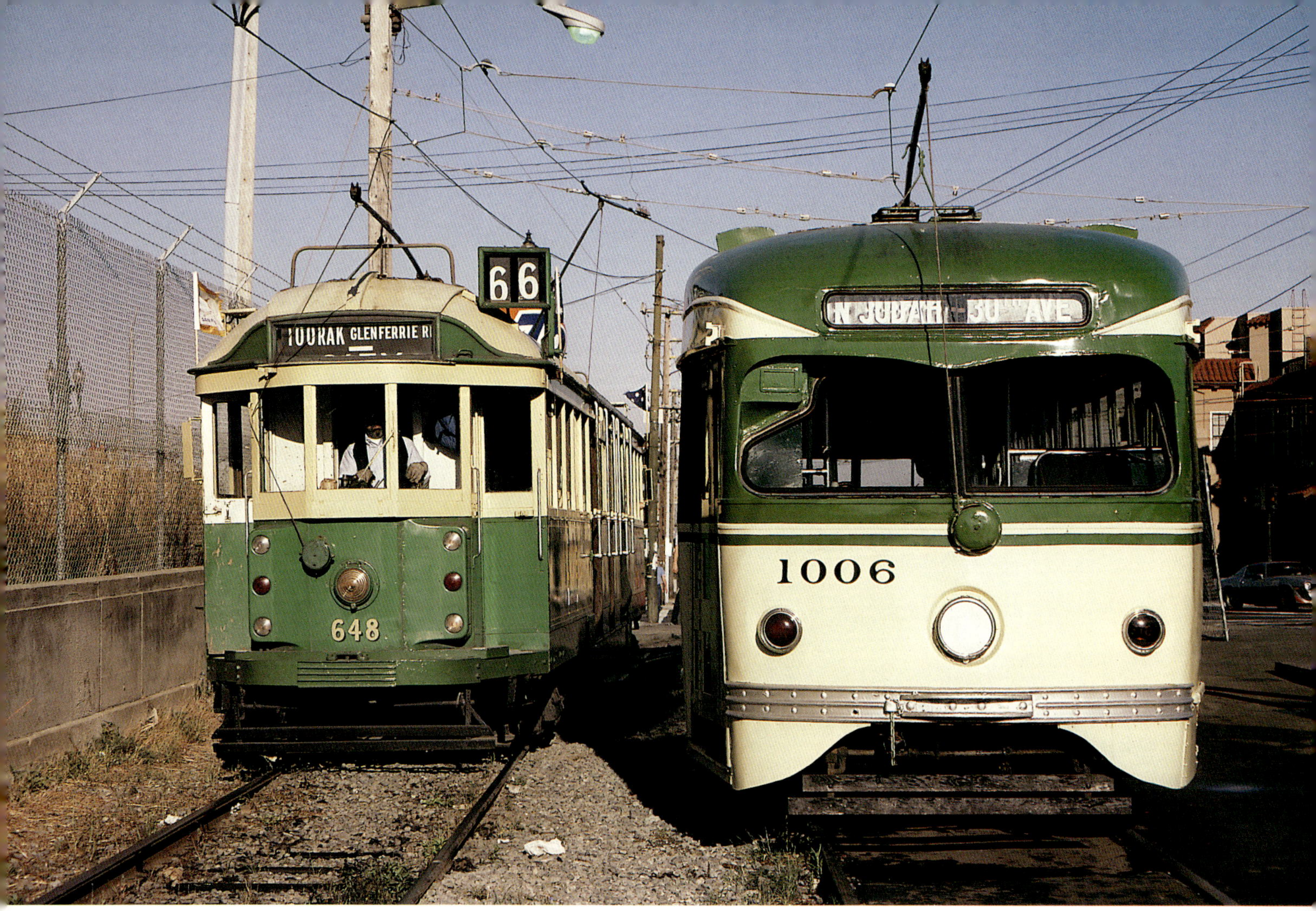

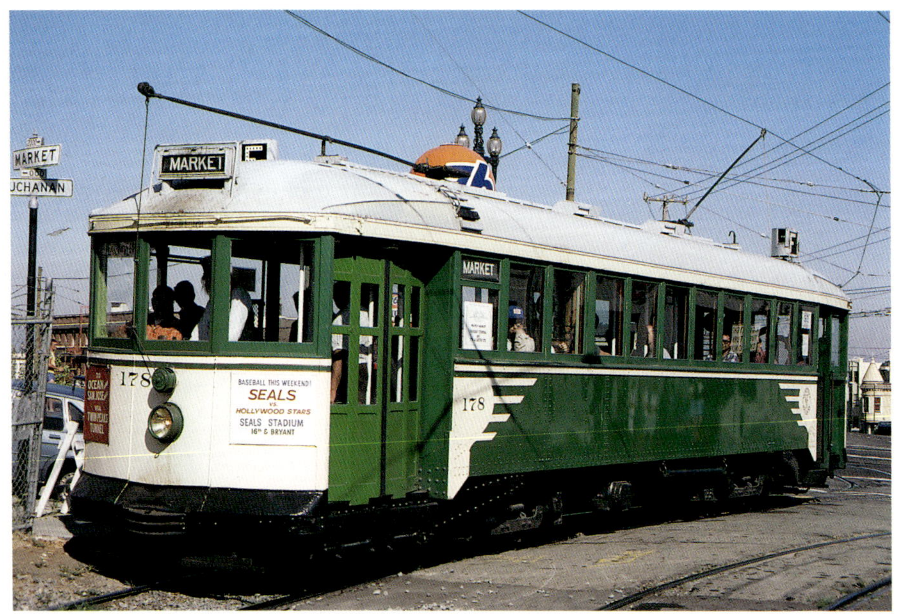

(ABOVE) Due to an increasing number of vehicles in use during Trolley Festival operations, single-tracking along the Duboce private-right-of-way allowed the inbound track adjacent to Mint Yard to serve as a car storage lane. Here, Melbourne No. 648, enroute to Castro Street, passes stored Muni P.C.C. No. 1006 in September 1984.

(LEFT) Municipal Railway type K streetcar No. 178, built by Bethlehem Shipbuilding Company in 1923, appears in the 1950-era Muni paint scheme as it stops to load passengers at Market Street and Duboce Avenue on September 16, 1984.

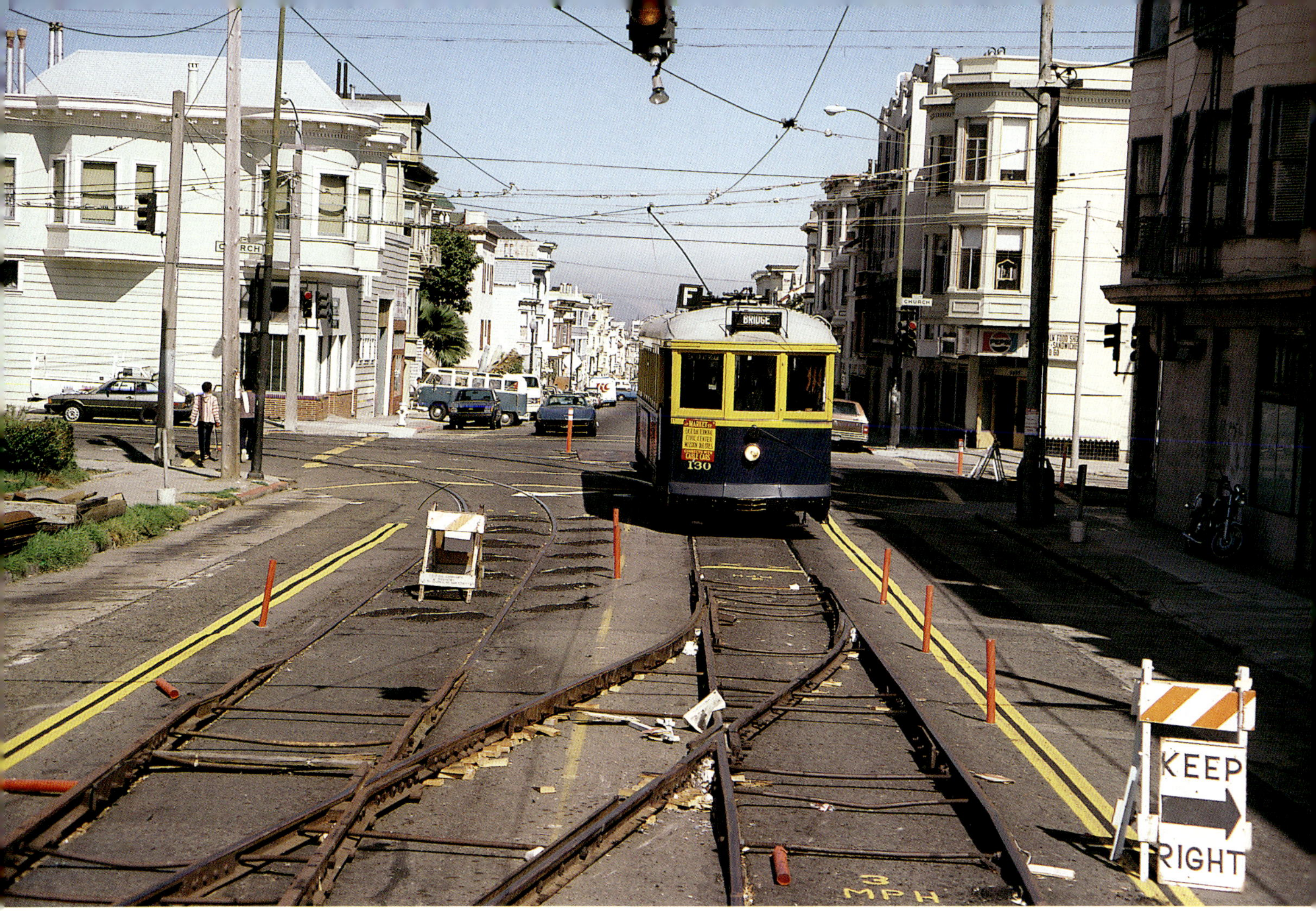

(ABOVE) During the re-railing of line "J" in Church Street, it was necessary to utilize portable crossovers to allow single-track operations to take place. Here we see car No. 130 turning westbound onto 17th Street, on August 26, 1984, during that construction process.
(RIGHT) Freshly painted, and still operated as a single-end car, Muni No. 1006 heads outbound on Market Street, just past 7th Street, in August 1984.

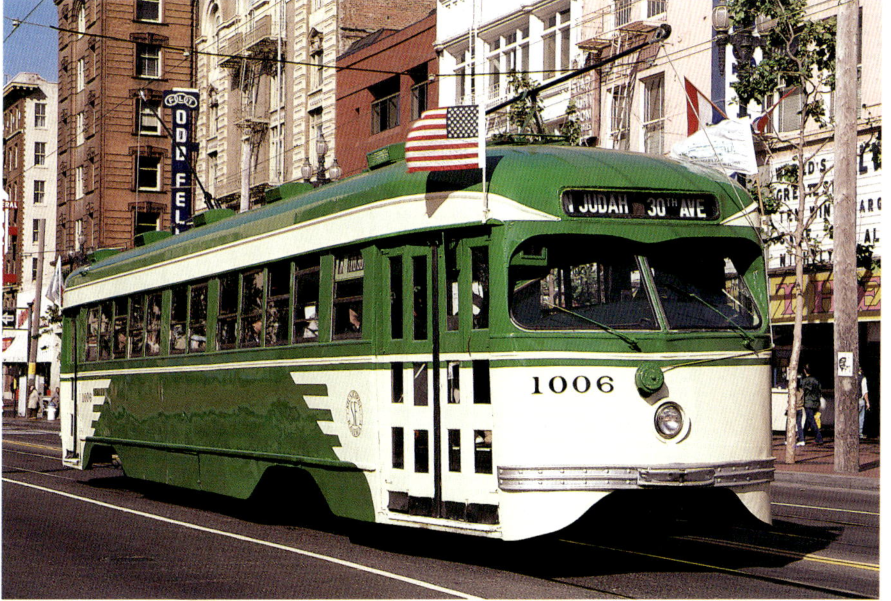

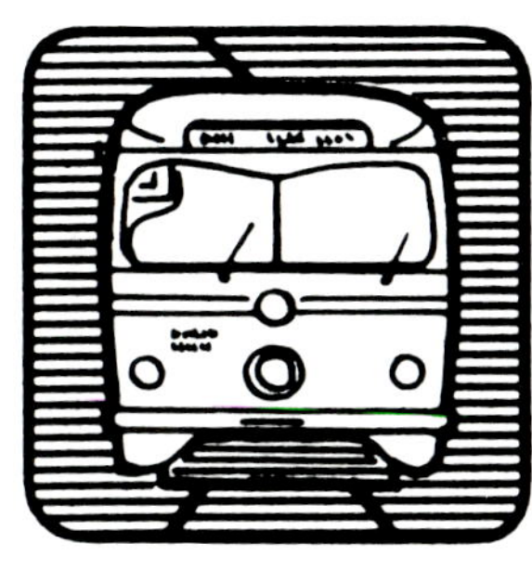

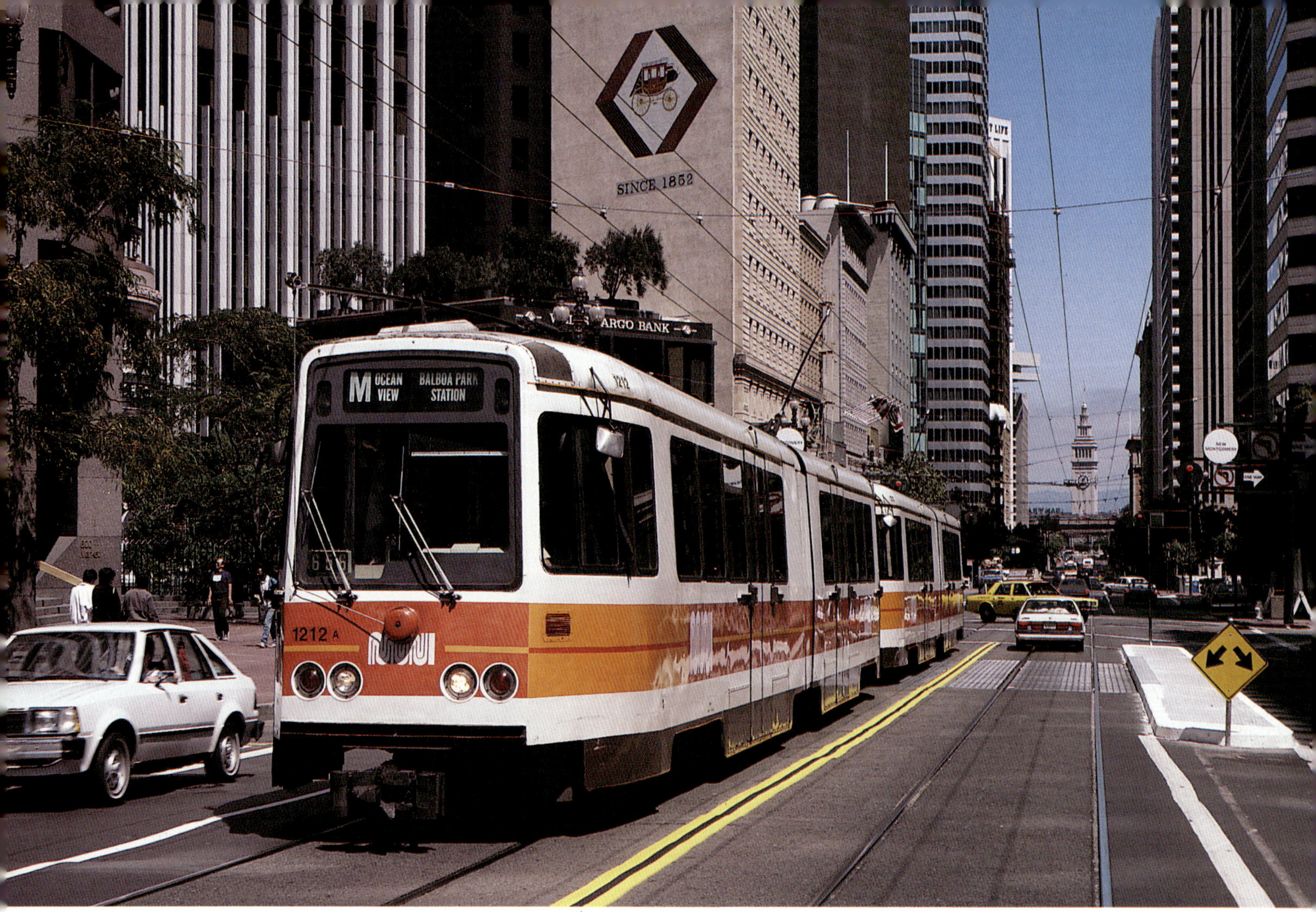

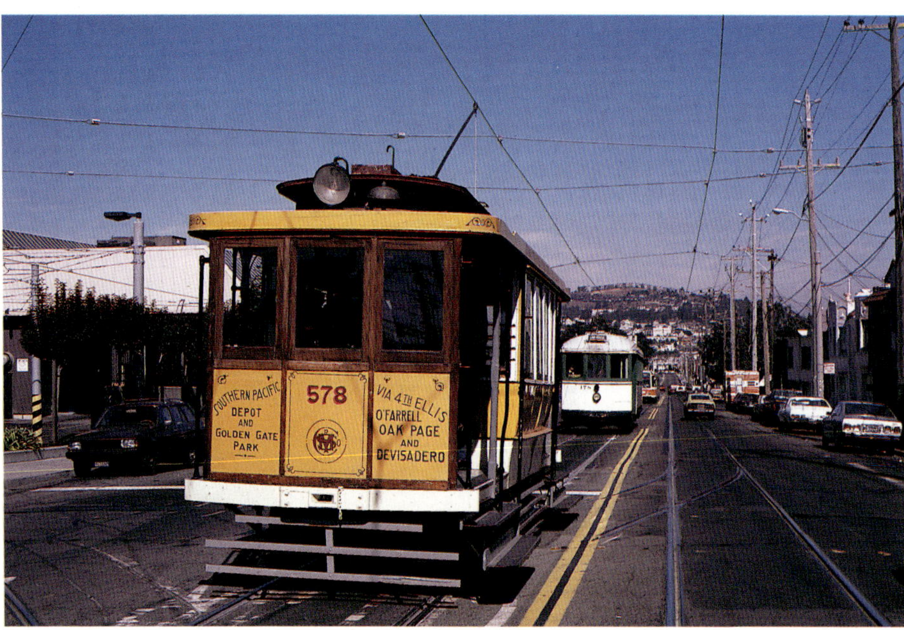

(ABOVE) Though not related to the Trolley Festival, a private charter of Muni's two trolley pole-equipped L.R.V.s on August 25, 1985, has been the only multiple-unit operation of those type of vehicles on lower Market Street's surface trackage to date. Here is that colorful train, southbound on Market Street at Montgomery Street, which consisted of cars No. 1213 and No. 1212. Motorman Harry D. Peat was the operator of this unusual consist.

(LEFT) Single-truck Market Street Railway car No. 578 was only an occasional Trolley Festival participant, due to the special handling necessary because of the car's lack of air brakes. Here we note that historic vehicle, on October 17, 1985, as it leads a parade of Trolley Festival cars down San Jose Avenue, to their winter storage at Geneva Yard.

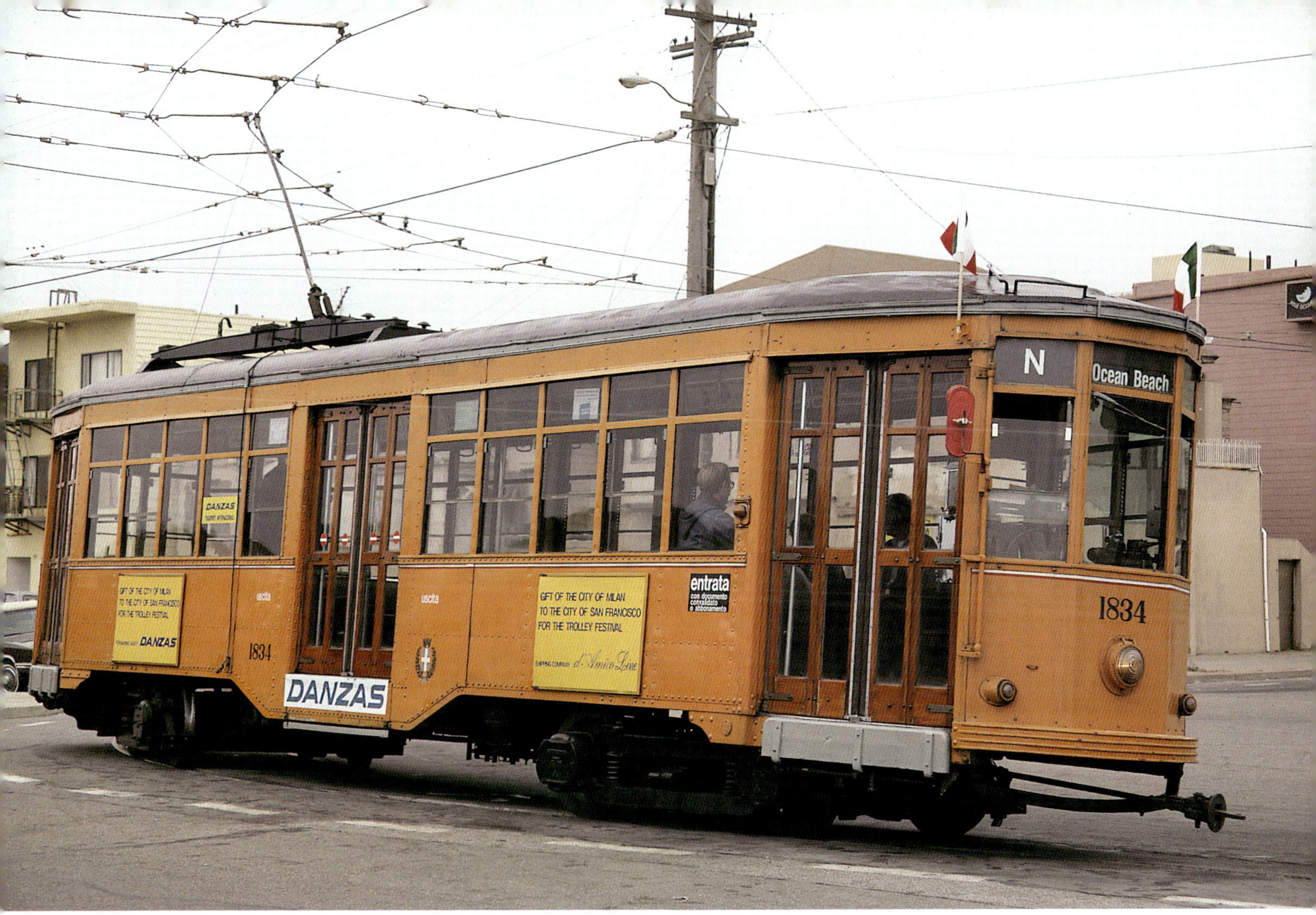

(ABOVE) Peter Witt-type car No. 1834, a gift to San Francisco from the citizens of Milano, Italy, is shown here at the beach terminal of line "N" on August 19, 1984. Fortunately for lovers of these vehicles, the Milano transit agency still operates over 300 of this type of car in regular daily service.

(RIGHT) This interior view of Milano No. 1834 shows the high standard of maintenance given its cars by the Italian city's transit authority.

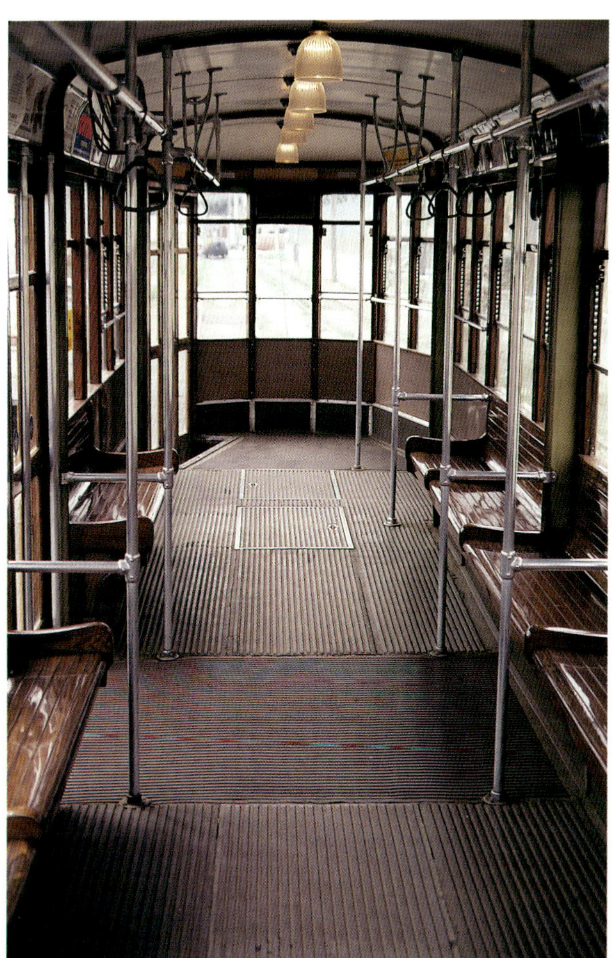

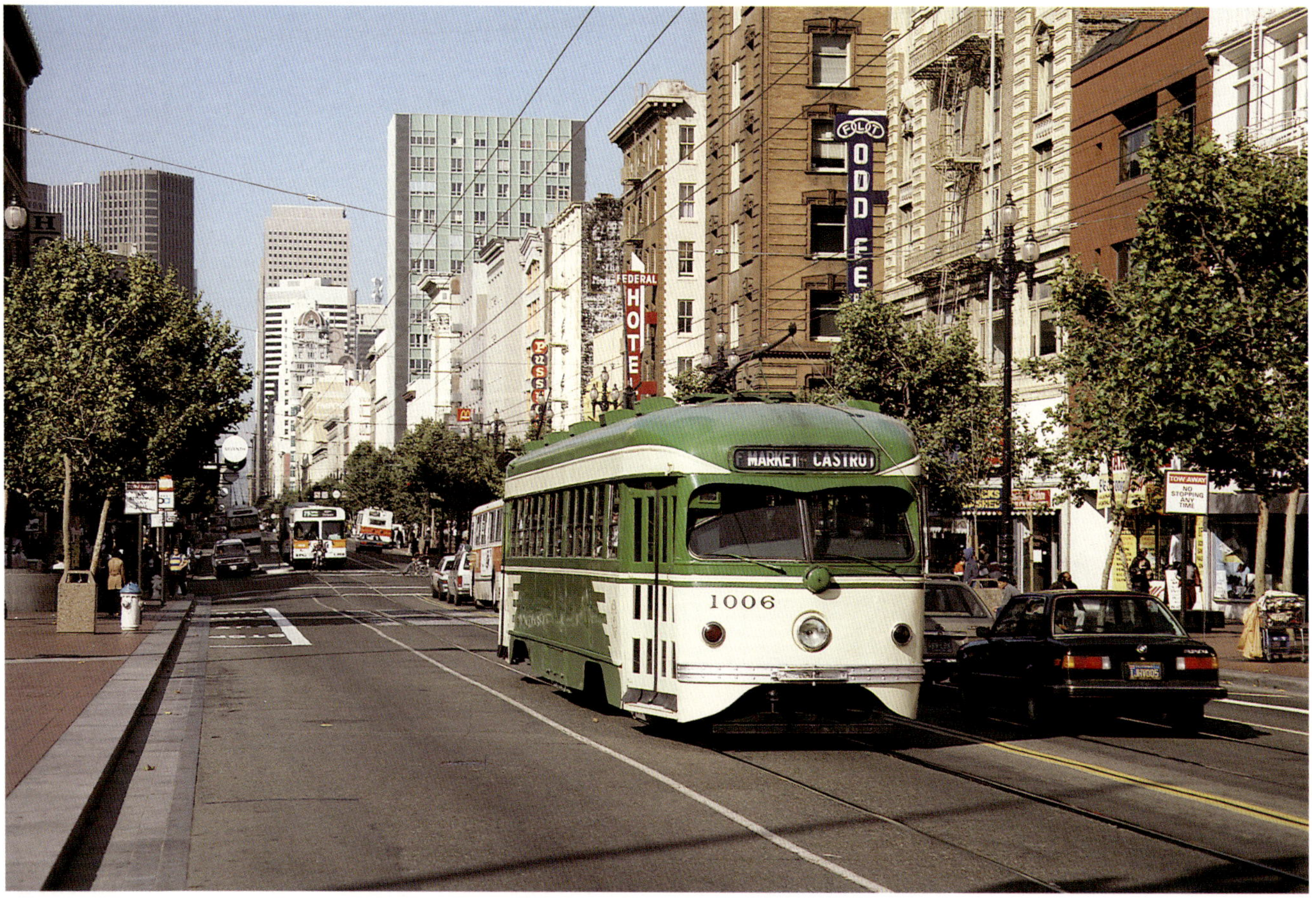

(ABOVE) Newly-restored to being a double-ended vehicle, P.C.C. car No. 1006 is seen southbound on Market Street, at 7th Street, on July 28, 1986. Known locally as "Torpedoes," these cars are 4 feet longer than Muni's single-end P.C.C. cars.
(BELOW) Here is another view of that classic transit vehicle as it is caught operating southbound on Church Street, just north of 17th Street, on October 17, 1986.

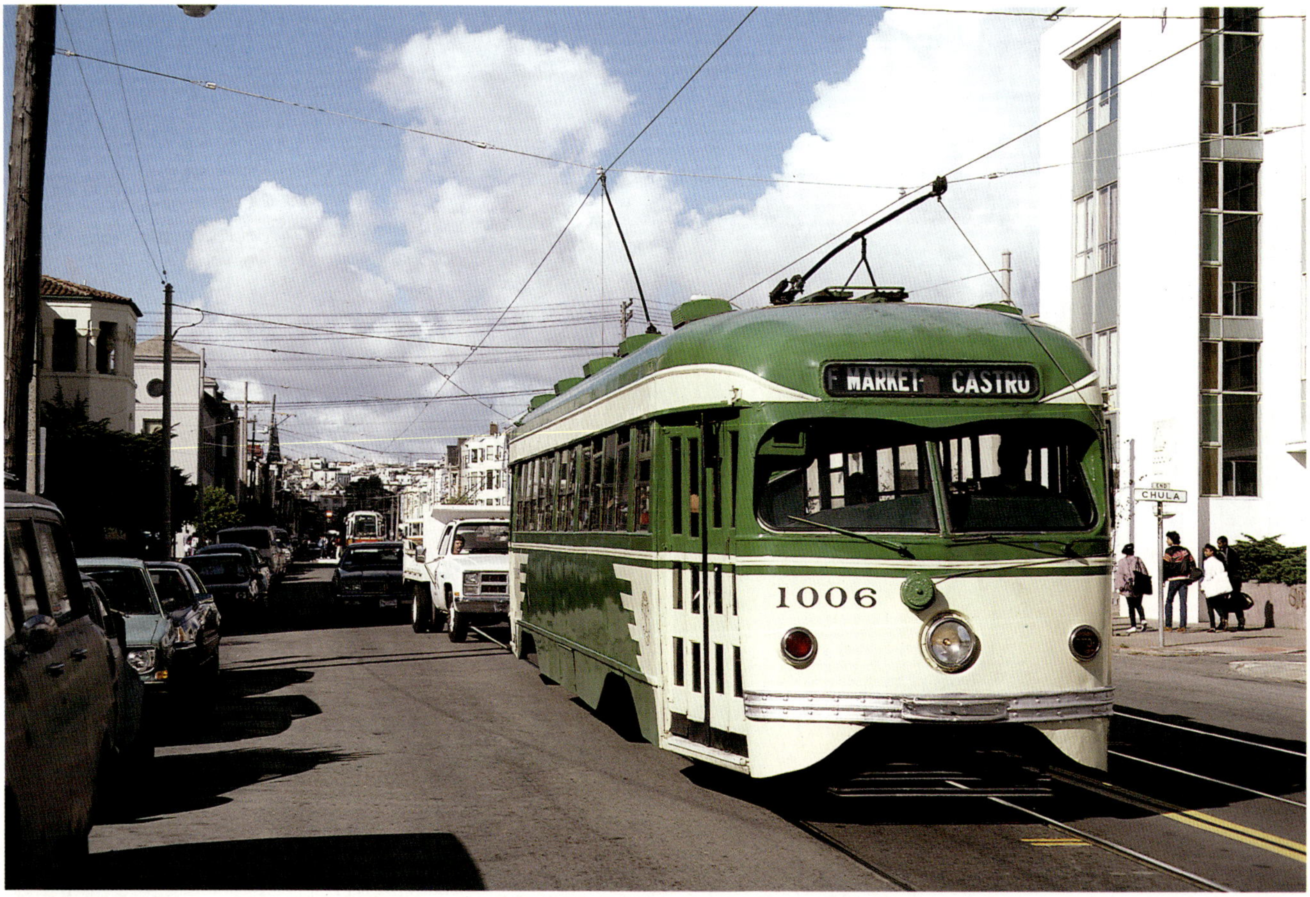

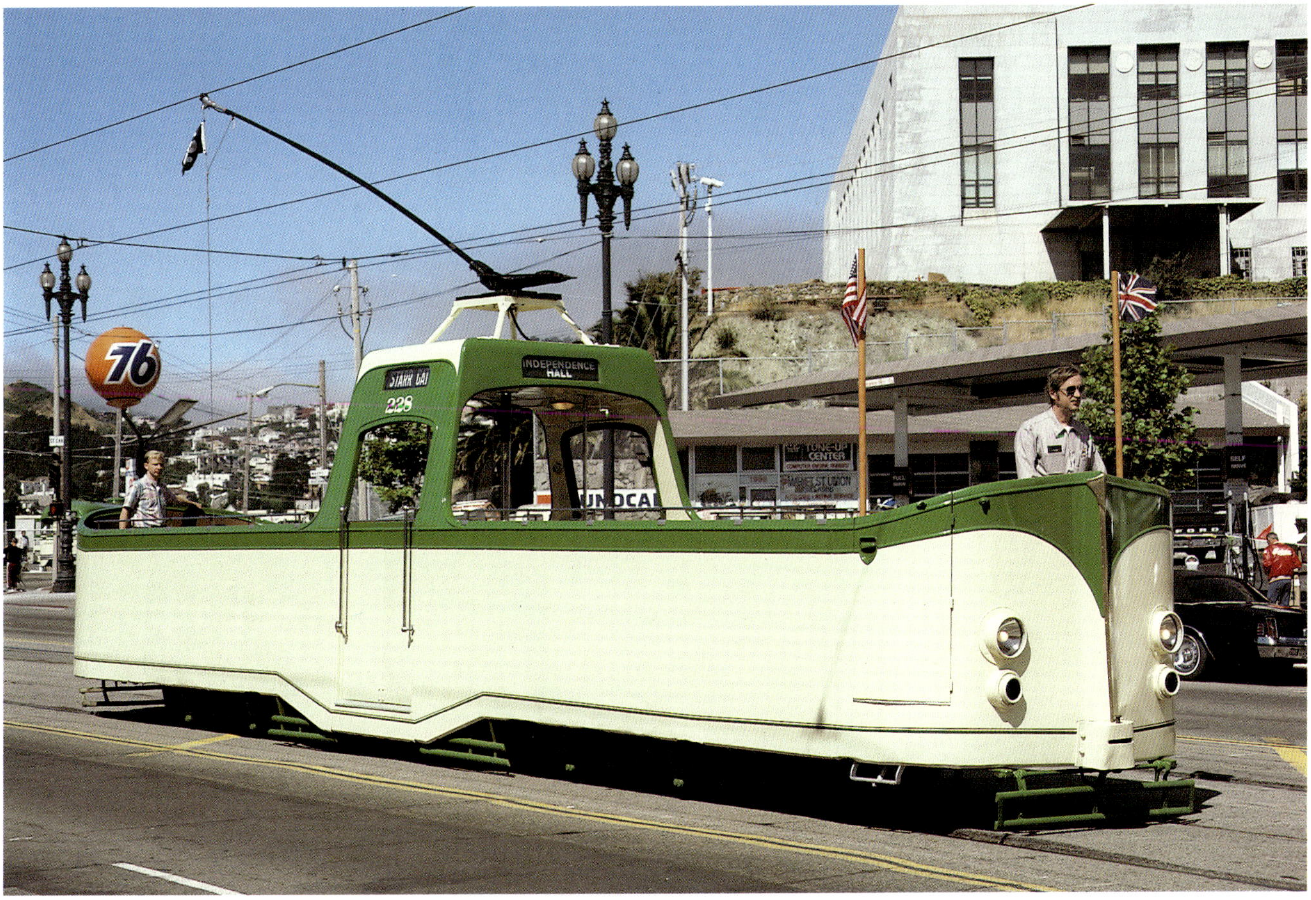

(ABOVE) Sent over from Blackpool, England, as a replacement for the Trolley Festival's original boat car, which was returned to its owner, No. 228 is photographed on Market Street, just north of Duboce Avenue, on May 26, 1986. **(BELOW)** Another gift to San Francisco, this time from Hiroshima, Japan, car No. 578 represents a typical type of tram car found upon many street railway systems in that country. In fact, this car was originally built for operation in Kobe, Japan, and in this view, taken at Geneva Yard on May 22, 1986, we see the car in its original single trolley pole configuration.

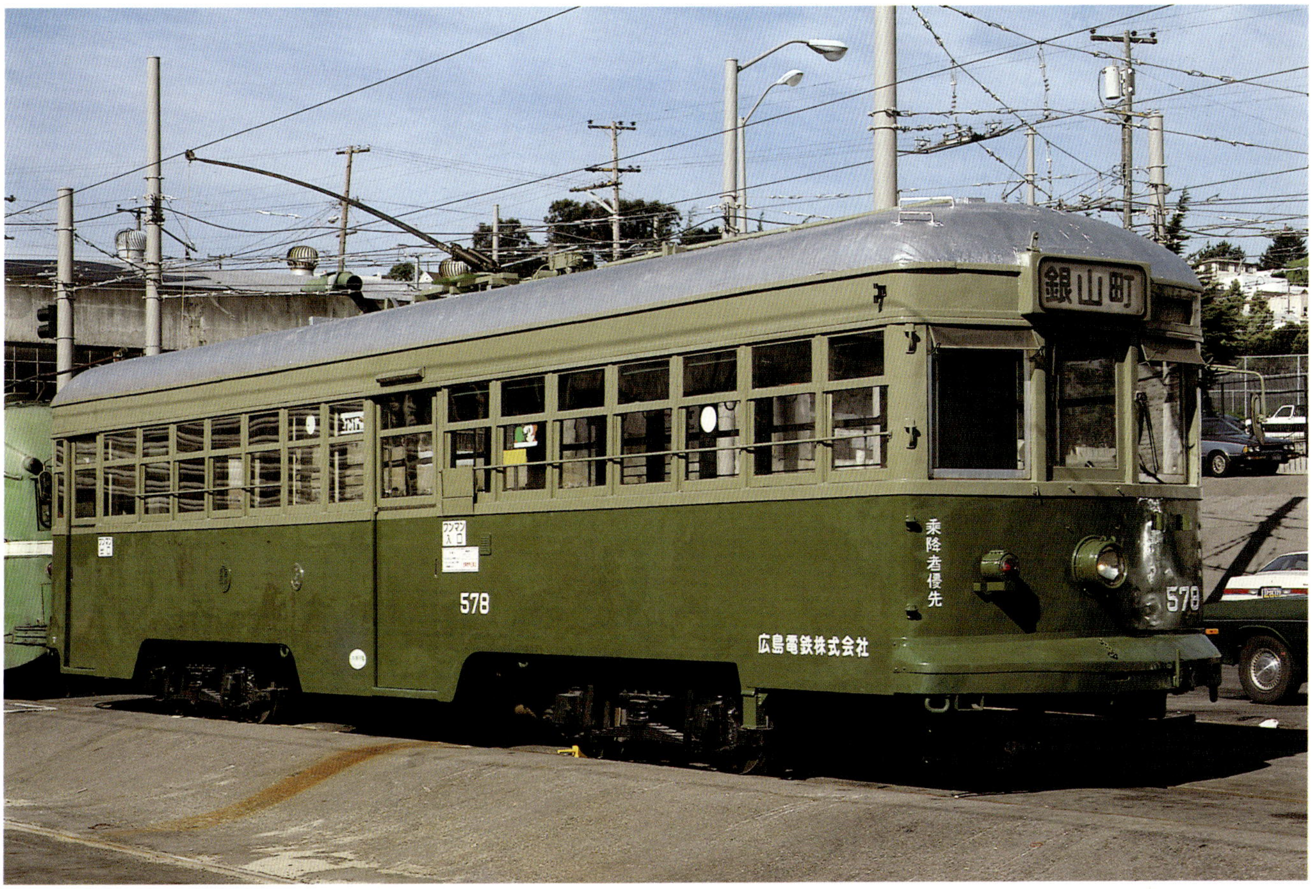

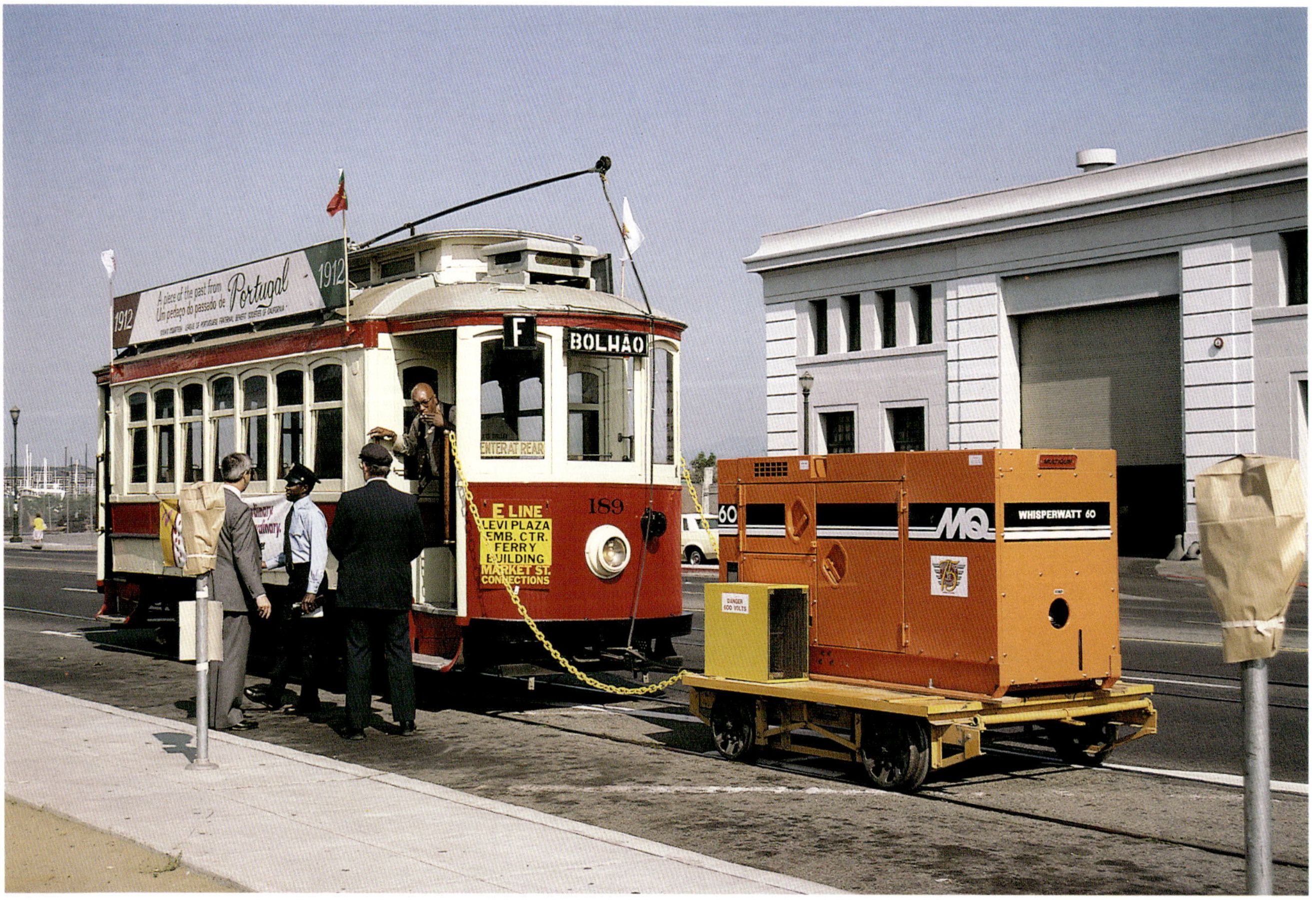

(ABOVE) During the summer of 1987, Trolley Festival operations were expanded to the city's northern waterfront with the addition of a two-car service between the Ferry Building, on the south, and Fisherman's Wharf, on the north. Here we witness Oporto No. 189, with its power-generating unit coupled on, about to begin its day's work on September 23, 1987.

(BELOW) A second Japanese tram car has been aquired for Trolley Festival operations. Shown here at the Metro Center storage yard, on December 3, 1987, is former Hankai Railway No. 151.

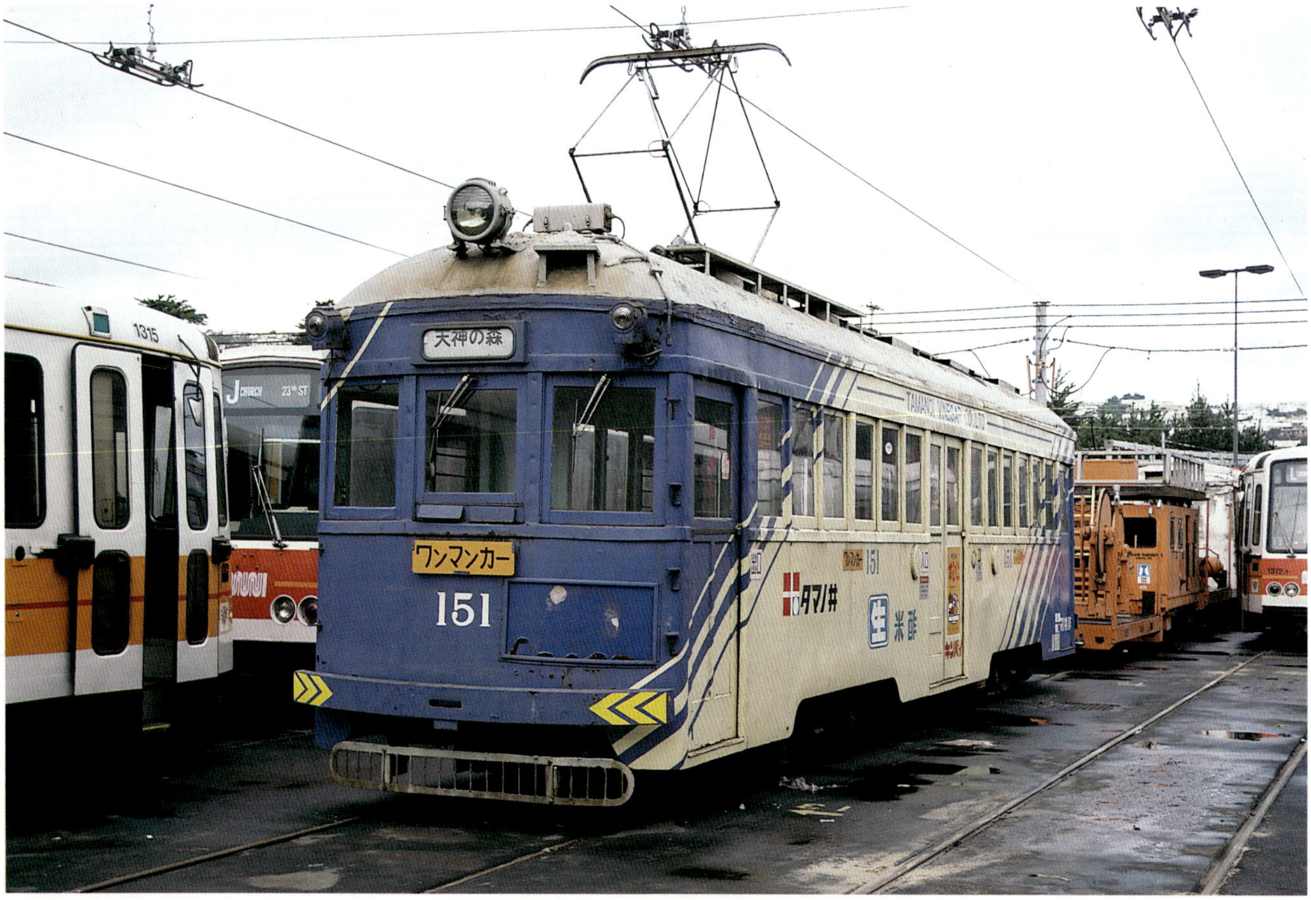

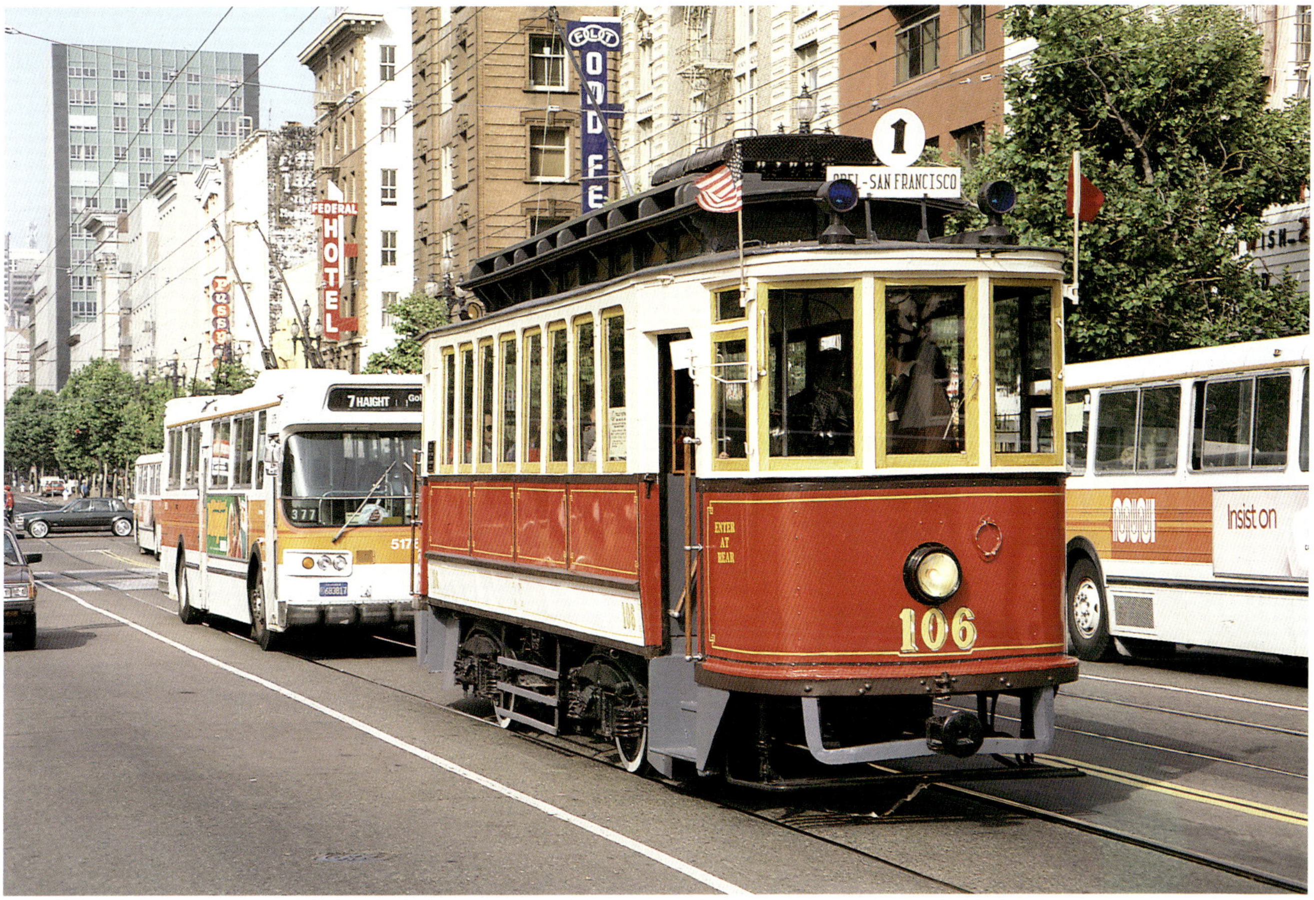

(ABOVE) Travelling over the seas from far-off Orel, Russia, U.S.S.R., is radial-truck-equipped car No. 106, another gift by a foreign country to the Trolley Festival operation. Shown here with comrade Jim Fine at the controls, we note car No. 106 southbound on Market Street, at 7th Street, on May 18, 1987.

(BELOW) Former Hiroshima car No. 578, seen here on Market Street, just south of Hermann Street on August 11, 1987, was rebuilt for double trolley pole operation during the shutdown period between the 1986 and 1987 Trolley Festivals.

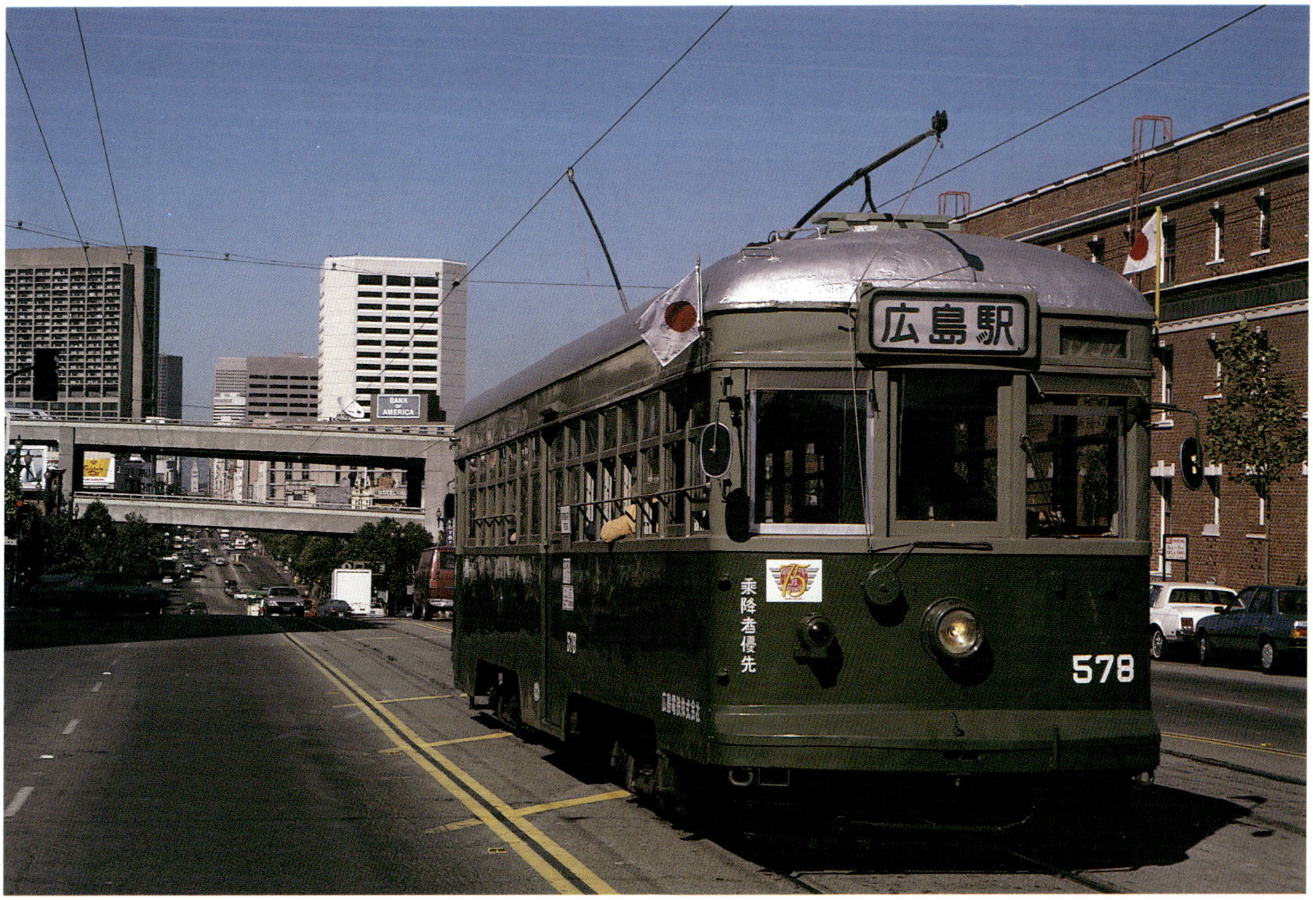

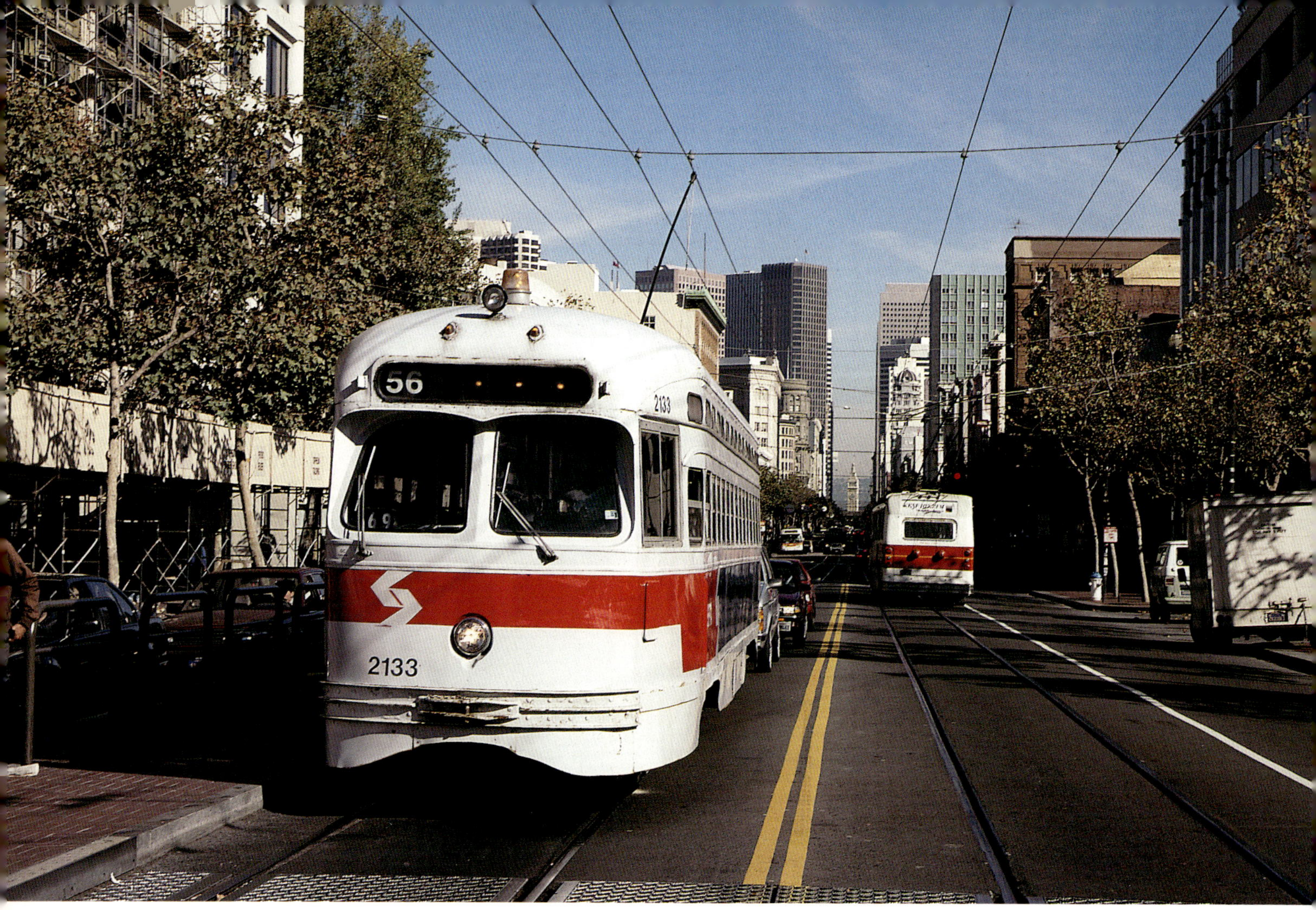

(ABOVE) The precursor of the rebuilt P.C.C. fleet, former Southeastern Pennsylvania Transportation Authority car No. 2133, is seen heading outbound on Market Street, at the 8th Street loading platform, on November 23, 1990, while on a non-revenue test run. This vehicle, which was received during the previous summer, was equipped with standard-gauge trucks from one of Muni's own 1016-1040-class P.C.C. cars, and was sent out in advance of other vehicles to allow specifications for the upcoming rebuilding project to be drawn up based on the observations of an actual car, rather than from vague generalizations. Plans now call for each of the rebuilt P.C.C. cars to be painted in the color scheme of other American cities that once operated the streamlined cars. Personally, I'm looking forward to the Pacific Electric Railway paint job-- I've always wanted to see a single-end P.E. P.C.C.!!
(OPPOSITE PAGE) To celebrate the completion of the rebuilding of the surface trackage on lower Market Street, a "mini" trolley festival was held on November 21, 1989. Here, outbound on Market Street, at Powell/5th Streets, is balloon-bedecked Orel car No. 106, with motorman David Strassman at the controls. As it travels down a broad thoroughfare rife with capitalistic enterprise, it is difficult to imagine that this handsome vehicle spent its entire working career transporting victims of a failed socialistic economy.

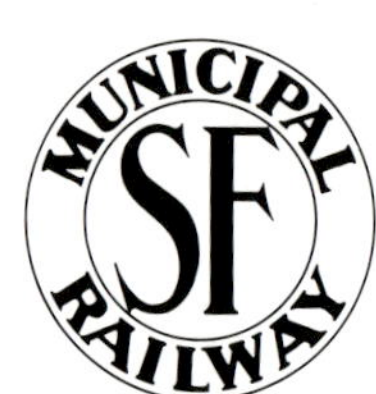

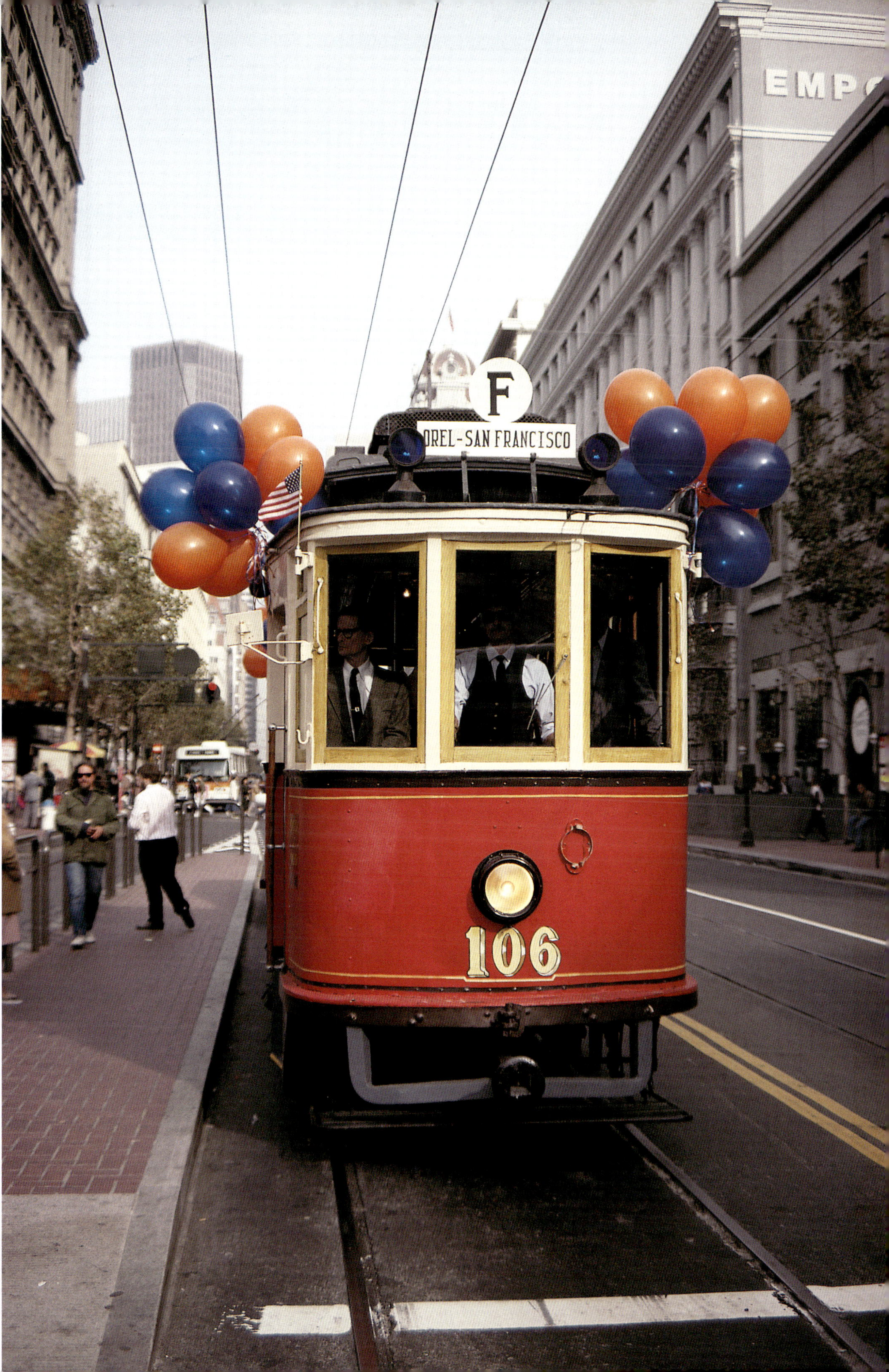
F
OREL-SAN FRANCISCO
106

ACKNOWLEDGEMENTS

Although the photographs reproduced within this album are all my own work, many wonderful and cooperative people helped to make these views possible. In many cases fellow workers posed vehicles especially for me, or allowed me to pose the vehicles myself. Many "test" runs were made with freshly-painted, or rebuilt, cars or buses, so that photographs could record those special events.

Therefore, I shall attempt to list some of the many employees of the San Francisco Municipal Railway who stand out in my memory as being especially helpful during the years of my employment by that concern; should I have overlooked someone, I ask their forgivness-- for my mind is slowly deteriorating from having viewed a few too many streetcar photographs over the years. I especially want to thank my working partner for the last 8 years of my Muni career, Mr. Anthony Camilleri, for tolerating my many demands and abuses as I subjected him to numerous photographic excursions.

Then there are also: Harry D. Peat, Jack Smith, James M. Cane, George Muscat, Bill Frost, Bob Olsen, Al Yee, Gerry Morelock, Kenny Rodriguez, Karl Johnson, Romer Manog, Art Michael, Jim Fine, Peter Ehrlich, Charlie Camilleri, Fred Holt, Tony Stellini, Marshall Moxom, Dick Forslund, John Nevin, Dennis McCoy, Ray Fontaine, Warren Demerrit, Nick Finck, Johnny Stein, Bob Higgins, Joe Batiste, Tom Biaggi, Chip Palmer, Larry Flynn, Lee Butler, George Horn, Larry Granfield, Art Curtis, Linda Trout, and Richard Morely.

Many Muni workers that have passed on to that great carbarn in the sky, and who were especially helpful over the years, were: the late Ray Davis, Charles Smallwood, Joe Slevin, Wally Leong, Robert McFarland, Emil Hausel, Ernie Scholtz, Dave Fay, Joe Shook, and Mike Wynkoop.

To all those listed above, and to countless other Muni employees, a sincere thank you for your contributions to this effort.

In addition, I thank my friend Cameron Beach, Chief Operating Officer of Sacramento, California's, Regional Transit District, and a native-born San Franciscan, for his invaluable editing and proof-reading services during the preparation of this work.

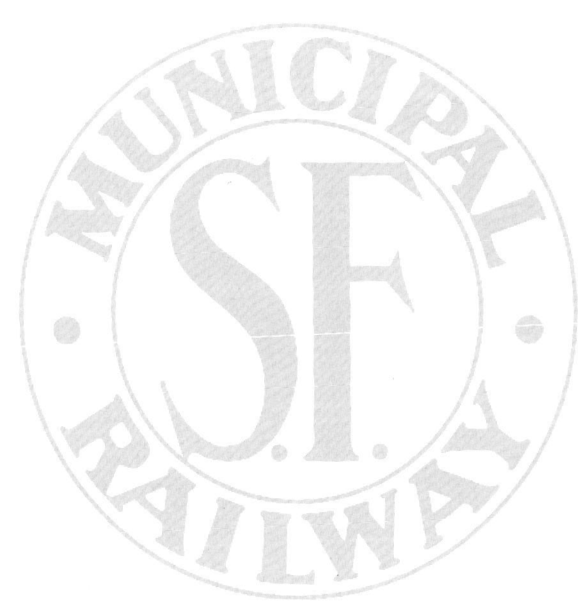